Frederick Wiseman

Frederick Wiseman

Edited by Joshua Siegel and
Marie-Christine de Navacelle

Contributors Andrew Delbanco   Geoffrey O'Brien
David Denby   Christopher Ricks
Pierre Legendre   Catherine Samie
Errol Morris   Joshua Siegel
Marie-Christine de Navacelle   William T. Vollmann
Jay Neugeboren   Frederick Wiseman

The Museum of Modern Art, New York

Gallimard

Frederick Wiseman is published in English and French editions by The Museum of Modern Art, New York, and Éditions Gallimard, Paris. The publication of the English edition coincides with an exhibition of all of Frederick Wiseman's films at The Museum of Modern Art throughout 2010.

Produced by the Department of Publications, The Museum of Modern Art, New York, and by Éditions Gallimard, Paris

English Edition
Edited by Kyle Bentley
Cover designed by Amanda Washburn
Published by The Museum of Modern Art, 11 W. 53 St., New York, New York 10019-5497 (www.moma.org)

Library of Congress Control Number: 2010932309
ISBN: 978-0-87070-791-9

Cover, front: *Welfare*. 1975. Back: *La Dernière Lettre* (*The Last Letter*). 2002

English edition distributed in the United States and Canada by D.A.P./Distributed Art Publishers, Inc., 155 Sixth Ave., New York, New York, 10013 (www.artbook.com). Distributed outside the United States and Canada by Thames & Hudson Ltd, 181 High Holborn, London WC1V 7QX, United Kingdom (www.thamesandhudson.com)

Printed in Spain

Un Certain Regard

Marie-Christine de Navacelle

Frederick Wiseman is a singular and solitary filmmaker. He explores, discovers, proposes . . . With moving images and recorded words, and without commentaries or interviews, he tells us stories that deliver a blow. Stories of our contemporaries going about their everyday lives, in all their humanity.

His cinema is no doubt one of the most perfect embodiments of what some of us in 1979 came to call *le cinéma du réel* (the cinema of the real) while creating the International Festival of Documentary Films at the Centre Pompidou in Paris. When he arrived that first year with *Sinai Field Mission* (1978), I found an *oncle d'Amérique* with big ears, piercing eyes, and a ravaging sense of humor.

It is this same man whom we now find at the Cannes Film Festival with *Boxing Gym* (2010), who has just shot a film about the Crazy Horse Saloon in Paris, and to whom The Museum of Modern Art is devoting a full-scale retrospective. It is this same man, still secretive and reserved—who prefers observing to being observed—who has agreed to present elements of his life and work to us, the painstaking work he considers a pleasure.

Wiseman is a lawyer by training but abandoned law in 1962, to his great relief, and five years later shot his first film, *Titicut Follies*, at the Bridgewater psychiatric prison near Boston. Leonardo DiCaprio said he watched the film to prepare for his role in Martin Scorsese's *Shutter Island* (2010).

Some speak of Wiseman with regard to Balzac, Dickens, Kafka, Beckett, and Ionesco—and he does recognize deep affinities with the last two—but his *comédie humaine* is one he has constructed himself relentlessly, with talent, acuity, sensitivity, and humor, as well as a tenacity that is specific to him. Above all, his work is a plunge into the core of contemporary American society by way of its institutions, hospitals, schools, army, and police. It is also an attentive look at his fellow citizens, a vision of America as a whole. He takes us to Texas, Alabama, Florida—through almost twenty states. Only two of his thirty-seven documentary films were shot in Boston, his place of birth, and eight in New York.

After years devoted to looking at the United States, he has since 1996 turned his attention toward

(Opposite) Frederick Wiseman by David Levine.
First appeared in the November 8, 1990,
issue of *The New York Review of Books*

Boxing Gym. 2010

adaptation of a chapter from Vasily Grossman's novel *Life and Fate* (1959)—and Samuel Beckett's *Oh les beaux jours* (*Happy Days*). He also made a fictional film of *La Dernière Lettre* with the actress Catherine Samie, who spent her entire career at the Comédie-Française, of which she was doyenne for several years. There she interpreted Molière, Marivaux, and Feydeau, as well as Shakespeare and Racine.

When The Museum of Modern Art chose to devote a retrospective to Frederick Wiseman, we thought that by working closely with the Museum, we could give the French as well as the American public the chance to discover or deepen their knowledge of Wiseman and his work.

We wanted to aid in a better understanding of this enigmatic, affable, demanding, and sometimes obstinate man, who is full of humor and sometimes irony. He is one of those rare filmmakers who produce, direct, edit, and distribute their films themselves. A tireless voyager, he crisscrosses the world to meet with his young and impassioned audiences. We also wanted to explore his exceptional relationship with literature and theater and to call on some of the people who have worked with him or have previously reflected on his body of work, whether critics, writers, philosophers, or artists.

France as well, a country with which he has long been familiar. He has chosen subjects that seemed to him to arise from very French specificities: the Comédie-Française, the Paris Opèra Ballet, and most recently the Crazy Horse, a Parisian cabaret where a revue by choreographer Philippe Decouflé was being unveiled. Wiseman made his Parisian debut in the theater (which like the ballet fascinates him), with stagings for the Comédie-Française of *La Dernière Lettre* (*The Last Letter*)—his

Wiseman's films have been shown all over the world, in festivals, museums, and art houses, at universities, and as well as on television. In France, the Cannes Film Festival presented *La Dernière Lettre* in 2002 and *Boxing Gym* in 2010. While the television broadcasts have allowed his films to reach new and diverse audiences, to penetrate into people's lives and homes, it is certainly on the big screen, in movie theaters (where *La Danse—Le Ballet de l'Opéra de Paris* [2009] met with considerable success) that the greatest number of people have been able to appreciate the force and beauty of his art.

More than is the case with much other work, the films of Frederick Wiseman speak for their maker, and this book invites the reader to see them and see them anew, going from astonishment to laughter, feeling the pleasure he takes in making them.

Translated from French by Jeanine Herman

Public Housing. 1997

Frederick Wiseman during the
filming of *Basic Training.* 1970

Inconclusion

Joshua Siegel

The effort really to see and really to represent is no idle business in face of the *constant* force that makes for muddlement. The great thing is indeed that the muddled state too is one of the very sharpest of the realities, that it also has color and form and character, has often in fact a broad and rich comicality.

—Henry James, *What Maisie Knew*[1]

The picture on the opposite page was taken in 1970 during the filming of *Basic Training*. Reporting for duty and armed to the hilt, Frederick Wiseman is a soldier in the army of gonzo-style New Journalism, standing ready to expose injustices and take down the powerful and the corrupt by any means necessary. The picture that appears on page six, by the visual satirist David Levine, portrays Wiseman as an exhibitionist-voyeur who pries into our private lives with a camera hidden inside his trench coat, in the place where his heart and soul should be. His smile is impish and his eyes are lidded with the weariness of someone who has seen it all before.

Both images are, of course, caricatures, but truth be told, Wiseman *has* seen it all before. He is a self-described "obsessive, fanatic fantasist." And as Catherine Samie and Errol Morris suggest in this book, he occasionally can be an avenging angel or a sly devil. This collection of original essays, by Wiseman himself and by eminent observers on both sides of the Atlantic, seeks to dispel persistent myths of Wiseman as a ruthless muckraker, a social worker, or a father of cinéma vérité. It offers a more nuanced, complicated, and open-ended portrait of him as one of the world's most fearless and innovative filmmakers.

For more than four decades, Wiseman has used a lightweight 16mm camera, synchronized sound equipment, and fast film stock to study human behavior in all its contradictory and unpredictable manifestations, particularly in institutional or regimented situations in which authority creates an imbalance of power, or where democracy is untidily at work. Like some great nineteenth-century novelists—Balzac, Hardy, George Eliot—Wiseman combines epic narrative with intimate portraiture. His films comprise a grand panorama of

American life and, more recently, the cultural life of Paris: a kind of modern-day *comédie humaine*. Wiseman approaches his breathtaking range of subjects—doctors, ballerinas, soldiers, students, welfare recipients, actors, factory workers, politicians, zookeepers, victims of domestic violence, corporate managers, fashion models, Benedictine monks, police officers, the terminally ill—with a minimum of intrusion or influence. He relies instead on a sensitive but trustworthy eye, a lawyer's penetrating skepticism, and the dramatic impulses of a storyteller to arrive at what Eugène Ionesco, one of his favorite playwrights, called an "imaginative truth."[2]

Wiseman's films never date. That's an astonishing achievement for any artist. Consider, for example, his film *Meat*, made in 1976, more than three decades ago. As we debate and agonize over the humane treatment of farm animals and the safety of our food, the future of family farms and the impact of agribusiness on the environment and on workers' rights, Wiseman's masterly study of one of America's largest feed lots and meat processing plants could not be more prescient or more provocative. *Meat* chronicles the journey of cattle and sheep from the auction block to the butcher block, tracing an automated system that is awesome in its effi- ciency and haunting in its implications about us as capitalist consumers. The dilemmas he poses in this film, and indeed in all of his films—moral, philosophical, legal, medical, technological, political, religious, and aesthetic— are as urgent and vexing as ever.

To ask ourselves *why* his films never lose their vitality or their currency would require us to speculate about how we have changed both as a society and as spectators during the past half-century. It would also require us to ask whether Wiseman himself has changed as a filmmaker. Wiseman refuses to go down that road. What he does do, in an essay written especially for this book and remarkable for its intimacy and illuminating detail, is to express his lifelong love of language, theater, books, good jokes and good conversation, and his appre- ciation of French culture. He considers, quite poignantly, the long shadow of war and the Holocaust, which have shaped his sensibility and his career. And he offers a lively and instructive account of what is involved in making his films.

It is left to the other contributors to present impressions, interpretations, and judgments of his work. Many of them do so in very personal ways. Andrew Delbanco describes his startling discovery of *Titicut*

Welfare. 1975

Follies (1967) as a student in the late 1960s, and how his experience of watching Wiseman's films, like the films themselves, has deepened and matured over time. If other writers like David Denby, Geoffrey O'Brien, and Jay Neugeboren also remember their discovery of Wiseman through *Titicut Follies*, and reflect on what O'Brien calls "the power of memory" as they revisit his other work, it is because Wiseman's first film still shocks and still shames. A landmark of nonfiction cinema, it is as grotesque a vision of human cruelty and suffering, of naked fear and loneliness, as art has ever produced, recalling the infernal torments of Goya's Black Paintings and Otto Dix's *Der Krieg* painting cycle.

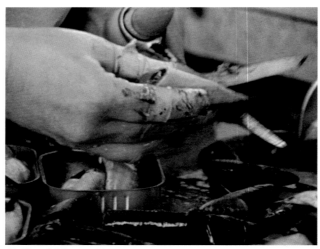

Belfast, Maine. 1999

Many authors in this book make reference to centuries-old paintings and poems. They comment on Wiseman's ear for language, and the way that conversations in his films always feel like extended monologues. (It is no wonder that Wiseman, David Slavitt, and Lenny Pickett would turn *Welfare*, Wiseman's 1975 "purgatorio" of bureaucratic and cosmicomic inertia, into an opera, drawing on the film's magnificent, aria-like lamentations.) Frequently they also praise the painterly beauty of his compositions, the way he photographs hands and faces and corridors and waiting rooms and towns at twilight, and the mysterious way he seems to give a *moral* dimension to everything inside the frame.

Perhaps more than any other artistic body of work, Wiseman's films stand as a monumental chronicle of late-twentieth-century institutional and cultural life. Describing *Belfast, Maine* (1999), Wiseman's meditation on American faith, resiliency, and industry, Delbanco concludes, "I suspect that future viewers will turn to this film as a documentary record of the United States in its late-industrial phase." Pierre Legendre observes, "The stars of his films are the institutions," later adding that "the question of what establishes law for man—the institutional imperative—is constantly inscribed in and traverses all of Wiseman's films." Ultimately these films endure because they transcend particularities of place, time, and character to reveal something profound about our common social existence and about the laws we impose or have imposed on us. William T. Vollmann writes, "As I explore Wiseman's oeuvre I come to expect revelations of littleness, and of the wastage of life, by life itself, or by people's incompetence, ineffectiveness, poverty, dullness—or by the regimentations and distortions entailed upon life by *process*." How often the people in his films seem to be killing time or delaying the inevitable, filling silences or wishing for nothing more than simply to be heard—wishing, as Denby writes, for someone to *give* them time.

This is the very essence of his films: the experience of time as a kind of vanitas, the imaginative arrangement of quotidian life as a reflection and a reminder of our own mortality. Pathos and irony, sorrow and pleasure, hope and despair not only coexist but also interact in intense, unpredictable ways. Christopher Ricks observes that "Wiseman's films make manifest both how much and how little cause we have to rejoice in this life." Yet Denby finds, "There is comfort in his films in the form of understanding, but you have to be strong to feel it. Let us call it comfort for the high-spirited and tough-minded." Comfort is a word that recurs throughout this book. Anger is another. Cold comfort, then, perhaps, but comfort nonetheless.

Joy, when it comes in Wiseman's films, comes rarely and is hard earned: the dancer and teacher Irina Kolpakova putting Susan Jaffe through her paces in *Ballet* (1995); the director Jean-Pierre Miquel rehearsing a production of Marivaux in *La Comédie-Française ou l'amour joué* (1996); Jason, the little boy in *Blind* (1986), making a difficult but triumphant solo journey between classrooms on different floors. Joy in these films is associated with dignity, freedom, and the creative act. And there is another kind of joy at work here: the evident joy that Wiseman takes in working. He works like a dog. Some of his most ecstatic moments, to use Catherine Samie's expression, are spent alone at the editing table laboring on his latest film, trying, as he puts it, "to find a form for my experience." An artisan who still cuts celluloid by hand, he makes countless choices as he inches through hundreds of hours of footage, letting the inherent rhythms of sound and image and the natural action of the creative process dictate the drama. Vollmann notes that "what we see in a Wiseman film has been edited, but gently; pulled up by the roots, but with the dirt left on."

The tones and sensibilities of the essays in this book are as richly varied as the films themselves, from irreverent to consoling to elegiac. One is reminded of the countless photographers and cameramen that Wiseman wryly films in the act of filming—in *Model* (1980), *Domestic Violence 2* (2002), and *State Legislature* (2006), to name a few—suggesting multiple vantage points and perspectives. "To summarize all that is going on in any one of these scenes would be the work of many pages, a whole volume perhaps," O'Brien concludes, "and no two observers would agree on what had been observed."

Things happen—the factness of the world—and we must marshal our imagination, compassion, and humility to cultivate a proper reading of them. Wiseman endeavors to do so, but like much powerful modernist art, his films are inconclusive. Samuel Beckett, an artist with whom Wiseman is often compared, wrote in his diary, "I am not interested in a 'unification' of the historical chaos any more than I am in the 'clarification' of the individual chaos, and still less in the anthropomor-

phisation of the inhuman necessities that provoke the chaos. What I want is the straws, flotsam, etc., names, dates, births and deaths, because that is all I can know."[3]

Wiseman does not offer any grand unified theories or tidy summations, either. Instead he gives us what O'Brien calls "a great book of instances," surmising, "What all those instances would add up to, in any given film and in the work as a whole, remains very much an open question." To use a metaphor so crucial to Wiseman's work, a documentary is a performance without a final curtain. The hunger of the imagination, our questioning, doubtful selves, can never be sated.

The essays in this book provide points of departure, avenues for further inquiry. There is much more to be said about Wiseman's depictions of faith and sacrifice, work, performance, the architecture of institutions, the fragility of our relationships to animals and to one another. As I write this, the eighty-year-old Wiseman is editing his two latest films, about a boxing gym in Austin, Texas, and the Crazy Horse Saloon in Paris. He has yet to stage his last play. He has yet to take his last shot. And the last word has yet to be written about him.

1. Henry James, *What Maisie Knew* (New York: Penguin Books, 1985), p. 30.

2. Eugène Ionesco, "Experience of the Theatre," 1958, in *Notes and Counter Notes: Writings on the Theatre*, trans. Donald Watson (New York: Grove Press, 1964), p. 16.

3. Samuel Beckett, German diaries, notebook 4, January 15, 1937, quoted in James Knowlson, *Damned to Fame: The Life of Samuel Beckett* (New York: Simon and Schuster, 1996), p. 228.

Ballet. 1995

Racetrack. 1985

A Sketch of a Life

Frederick Wiseman

"Who are you?" said the Caterpillar.

This was not an encouraging opening for a conversation. Alice replied, rather shyly,

"I–I hardly know, Sir, just at present–at least I know who I was when I got up this morning,
but I think I must have been changed several times since then."

"What do you mean by that?" said the Caterpillar, sternly. "Explain yourself!"

"I can't explain *myself*, I'm afraid, Sir," said Alice, "because I'm not myself, you see."

"I don't see," said the Caterpillar.

"I'm afraid I ca'n't put it more clearly," Alice replied, very politely, "for I ca'n't understand
it myself, to begin with; and being so many different sizes in a day is very confusing."

"It isn't," said the Caterpillar.

"Well, perhaps you haven't found it so yet," said Alice; "but when you have to turn into
a chrysalis–you will some day, you know–and then after that into a butterfly, I should
think you'll feel it a little queer, wo'n't you?"

"Not a bit," said the Caterpillar.

"Well, perhaps your feelings may be different," said Alice: "all I know is, it would feel
very queer to me."

"You!" said the Caterpillar contemptuously. "Who are you?"

Which brought them back again to the beginning of the conversation.

–Lewis Carroll, *Alice's Adventures in Wonderland* [1]

Introduction

I do not like to write about myself or my films. I am not sure I understand the films and I know that I do not understand myself. Since I cannot or will not try to explain my films or myself or write about my immediate family, this essay for a book about my films presents a problem for me. However, I am very pleased to have a distinguished group of writers commenting on my films. In this essay I will try to offer some personal history that may or may not be related to my career as a filmmaker, followed by brief accounts of what is involved in obtaining permission for, researching, shooting, editing, financing, and marketing a film.

Autobiographical Notes

One theory I have about myself is that I am a fantasist, a word that has some letters in common with "fanatic." Maybe I am a fanatic fantasist. "Fanatic" implies obsessive. Therefore, maybe I am an obsessive, fanatic fantasist. In any case I like to work hard and constantly. Making a lot of films has certainly made it easier for my compulsive work habits to find a form. Perhaps if I did not have work that I like I would wash my hands all day or do something even more obviously clinically identifiable.

Instead I make films. And I like to call them films rather than documentaries. I think they are structured stories with a beginning, a middle, and an end and with some elements in common with feature films and other forms of fiction. They are not documents explaining the social structure of a community.

I did not always work hard. In grammar school and high school I spent most of my time looking out the window and avoiding contact with teachers, most of whom reciprocated my dislike and discomfort. I was a sort of Artful Dodger, which I now, in my maturity, realize might have been a mistake. If I had managed to pay attention I might have gotten a better formal education instead of enduring twenty-one years of schooling only to end up basically self-taught. In grammar school and high school I could not concentrate on anything except my daydreams, although I am not sure I knew enough to call them daydreams. I knew that I was bored but was not smart enough to try to find someone who could reassure me or offer some comfort to the anxious state the boredom inflicted. Back then the obsession took the form of sports. Football in the fall, hockey in the winter, tennis and baseball in the spring and summer. I, like many of my math-challenged friends, could recite baseball statistics back to the beginning of time, which was the beginning of baseball. If someone had given a class on how to design a baseball card I would at least have had one good grade in grammar school. One of the great tragedies of my life was that my mother threw out all my baseball cards when I went off to college, among them the Honus Wagner card which someone years later bought at an auction for $475,000, or so *The New York Times* reported. I never found out if the seller was the person who collected garbage from our house.

I grew up listening to World War II on the radio. My father was a lawyer in Boston but used his legal training to help immigrants from Europe, particularly Jews escaping to America from anti-Semitism and war. He had emigrated to the United States as a Russian-born five-year-old in 1890. He never talked about his first five years in Russia and concentrated on becoming an American, an active and responsible member of the community. The community in those days was the Jewish community since anti-Semitism was everywhere, or so it felt to me who remembers listening to Hitler's speeches on the radio and the rants of Father Coughlin, a Roman Catholic priest who regularly raged against Jews on a Sunday morning radio program broadcast nationwide. In the 1930s in Boston it was almost impossible for a Jew to be a member of a Yankee law firm or to have a staff position at a Boston hospital. Most Jews lived in their ghetto. The Irish and Italian fellow immigrants lived in their own separate ghettos. All were treated as second-class citizens by the dominant New England Yankee society. There was a lot of talk at home about ethnic differences, rivalries, and hatred, and as war approached I became slightly more aware of the link between what was going on in Europe and Asia and the political conflicts in America. From 1938 on, we listened to the news at night during dinner and my parents made great efforts to explain to me the world outside the house.

My father was quite knowledgeable and aware about politics. My mother considerably less so. She always wanted to be an actress and was accepted to the American National Theatre and Academy in 1917 at the age of seventeen but her father refused to let her go because he believed that actresses were all whores and his beautiful daughter was not to be allowed to join that sorority. She never quite recovered from his refusal, and that, perhaps, is the origin of my career as a filmmaker (which is not to suggest that all filmmakers are whores). A frustrated actress, she brought theater home. Almost every afternoon when I returned from school, she would imitate all the people she had met during the day. She could look and listen to someone for twenty seconds and then render a perfect imitation that was funnier than anything I saw at the movies, and there was a lot of competition from the Marx Brothers, Charlie Chaplin, the Ritz Brothers, W. C. Fields, and Laurel and Hardy. They were funny but not as immediately funny as the cast of characters brought home each day from my mother's ramblings around the city. She introduced me to antique dealers, jewelry salesmen, streetcar conductors, window washers, used car salesmen, secretaries, real estate agents, delicatessen counter men, grocers, butchers, chicken farmers, bored middle-class women, and whomever else she met in the course of the day. Her range of material increased considerably when she began to work as the administrative head of the first psychoanalytically oriented childcare center in the United States. The cofounders were Marian Putnam, the daughter of James Jackson Putnam, the doctor who first brought Freud to the United States, and Beata Rank, one of the serial wives of Otto Rank, an early disciple of Freud who later separated from the master. Mrs. Rank was birdlike in physique with a quick, mean, and acid tongue and Marian Putnam

was kind, gentle, and equally intelligent. One of the first plays I ever saw was my mother's imitation of an argument between these two titans of the early American psychoanalytic world. She did both parts brilliantly. I had met both women and her re-creation went right to the core. I vividly remember her imitating the conversation between them about whether identical twins who thought they were birds could fly. So it was then and there in 1939 that I decided to make movies based on real experience, although I was, then, unaware of my decision. The only movies I had seen with people who were not actors were the *March of Time* newsreels that I watched every Saturday afternoon at the neighborhood theater I religiously attended. When World War II started, this was also my way, along with the nightly radio broadcasts, of following the war. Some twenty-seven years later I made my first film, thus documenting what everybody knew about me and worried about on my behalf—namely, that I was a slow learner.

I daydreamed my way through high school. Almost the only strong memory I have is hitting three triples in one game against our archrivals. For fifteen or twenty minutes I was sure a career in major league baseball awaited me on graduation. However, I was soon put in the difficult situation of having to choose which sport would lead me to fame and fortune. I lost in the finals of the first grass-court tennis tournament in which I was playing but having reached the finals I was sure that those pros at the top of their game would soon have to make room for me. My only intellectual triumph was winning the *Time* magazine current events quiz in 1943 (a local—very local—not national winner). I have no memory of thinking that this triumph would propel me to the top ranks of politicians or political scientists. This perhaps represented one of the limits of my fantasy life and served as yet another indication of my not wanting to grow up.

College is also a blur. I went to Williams, a good small college. Good in the sense that it had a fine faculty. Bad because it was representative of those many colleges in the United States that even after World War II (I enrolled in 1947) were examples of institutionalized anti-Semitism. The social life was built around fraternities. Jews were not admitted except those few who successfully concealed their religious origins. The Jews and other misfits were huddled together in a group of dormitories and ate in a common dining room largely cut off from the social life of the rest of the campus. Some of my Jewish classmates were not bothered by this.

I was. My innocence rebelled at the unfairness and one consequence was that, after fitfully enduring this discrimination for the first two years and not being able to make sense of the unhappiness that it caused, I began for the first time in my life to read. I found my way to a poetry seminar on Yeats, Pound, Eliot, and Stevens taught by a professor who demanded of his students that they learn how to read with care and attention. I became aware of words as conscious choices, not just as sounds that rolled out of one of the openings between my ears. While my hatred of Williams and all that it represented socially remained, my late-blooming interest in reading propelled me through the last two years of college and three years of law school.

I went to Yale Law School because I did not know what else to do, and besides, if I did not attend some professional graduate school, I would have been drafted into the army and sent to fight in Korea. Even law school seemed to be, to my keen analytical mind, a better alternative than going to war. At law school I studied for the first semester because I was scared. The first day of law school, when the class was assembled for an orientation, the dean's welcoming remarks were almost drowned out by the jingling of Phi Beta Kappa keys ostentatiously displayed, even though none were, then, hung from noses or pierced lips. I was always puzzled as to how I was allowed to join this distinguished group since I had no key (or clue) and was nervous as to whether I could compete with such accomplished colleagues.

I discovered that the close reading I had been taught in poetry seminars was the skill I needed to survive in law school. At college I had learned that I had an appreciation of the formal beauty and ambiguity of language. I quickly turned this into a reason not to study at law school. After my intensive and rewarding reading of great poetry, the pedestrian language of appellate court decisions was just plain boring, no matter how important the question the case posed. Reading appellate court decisions was punishment that I could avoid by going to the university library, fortunately located just across the street from the law school, where every novel, poem, or play that anybody would want to read was available on open shelves. Strategically placed around the reading rooms were sinfully comfortable chairs. In brief, I was in reader heaven. Thus passed the next two and a half years of law school. Friends lent me notes and recommended last-minute reading and the key to passing was to go to bed early the night before the exam so that I could approach the blank pages of the exam book with an empty but clear mind which allowed me to play with the language of the questions with barely enough knowledge of the law to muddle through.

After law school the Korean War was over but the army still needed me. I survived basic training and clerk typist school. I was assigned to the judge advocate general's office at Fort Benning, Georgia, and managed to get sent on to court reporter school at the University of Virginia. This lush assignment of six weeks meant that I did not have to go on a maneuver in the Louisiana swamps filled with rattlesnakes that fed on soldier meat. After my training, I spent my days repeating every word uttered by defense and prosecution counsel, witnesses, defendants, and the members of the court martial into a gas mask that had been adapted to hold a microphone. The mask was necessary so that my repeating of all the speech at the trial would not be heard and would not disturb the participants. I became skilled at repeating anything anybody said. This turned out to be a great party trick. When I was bored with others I could silently repeat their conversations to myself, and if I wanted to annoy people I would repeat whatever they said with a two-second delay. This, as it accidentally turned out, was very useful years later in recording sound, since most film tape recorders allow you to listen to the recorded sound with a two-second delay. I thus had the skill of both listening and repeating with a two-second delay.

My final six months in the army were spent reviewing fraudulent contracts. Hundreds of people, who clearly suffered from a lack of patriotism, were accused of trying to cheat the army on contracts for uniforms. They either had not used the correct materials or had delivered less than was agreed on. This was too much like law school for me, but I managed to avoid some of the tedium by taking long absences related to real or imagined illnesses. The beaches of Cape Cod greatly aided my recovery. One time I was away for so long that when I reported back for duty the uniform had changed. This led to my presence and therefore my absence being noted, since my shoes and pants were no longer the right color. In 1956 it was possible to be discharged from the army three months early if you went to school. I scoured the world for a school that started on November 1 and found that the Faculty of Law at the Sorbonne did. My application was accepted and I was discharged from the army to study at the Sorbonne. I followed my usual pattern and did not

La Comédie-Française ou l'amour joué. 1996

attend any of the law classes. Instead I began to learn French. A project that has continued to this day, fifty-four years later.

The GI bill was enough to live on and Paris was a lark—student restaurants, last-minute discount tickets to the Comédie-Française, the Compagnie Renaud-Barrault, the Théâtre National Populaire of Jean Vilar, cheap, good food and wine, and all the great movies past and present. My wife and I went to the movies or the theater almost every day or night. I went through my Fitzgerald and Hemingway phase without writing a word, although once I sat in the café Les Deux Magots ostentatiously reading *What is Existentialism?* by Jean-Paul Sartre. Unwittingly, in Paris, I was continuing my education, but I was professionally as directionless as ever. I shot several 8mm movies principally of my wife shopping on the Rue des Martyrs. This, I recognize retrospectively, was part of my mindless grope toward a career. More or less unconsciously I was continuing my lifelong process of self-education. After twenty-one months my cliché expat time in Paris was over, and I went back to Boston to start a real career. I do not know how to avoid nor do I wish to enlarge this banal summary of my time in Paris. I learned a lot and did not do much.

I went back to Boston and found a job teaching at Boston University School of Law. My subjects were legal writing, legal medicine, family law, and copyright. I knew next to nothing about any of these subjects but from the law school's point of view I was a cheap hire, and for me it was yet another chance to prove I was a quick study. I never inquired whether the students felt cheated.

I tried to make the course in legal medicine interesting for the students and myself by introducing some reality other than dry, poorly written appellate court decisions. Many of the students from Boston University went on to careers as criminal lawyers or district attorneys. I thought they should know the kinds of places defendants would end up in if they were poorly represented or overzealously prosecuted. So I arranged field trips to prisons, parole board hearings, mental hospitals, trials, medical examiners' offices, and social welfare agencies. One of the institutions I visited with the students was the Massachusetts Correctional Institute at Bridgewater, or as it was then known, MCI Bridgewater. Bridgewater was a maximum-security prison divided into four sections—the criminally insane, alcoholics, defective delinquents (I still do not know what this means), and sexual offenders. We visited all four sections and met the correctional staff, the prison doctors, the administrators, and many inmates. In three years I visited Bridgewater perhaps five times. In arranging those visits I became friendly with the superintendent. This friendship would eventually lead to the making of my first film, *Titicut Follies* (1967).

In 1961 my fringe interest in movies began to push its way through the maze of my mind. I had read Warren Miller's novel *The Cool World* (1959). The novel was about teenage gangs in Harlem, drug dealers, and generally about being poor and black in New York. All of what became the standard portrayals of black life were present in *The Cool World*, but Warren Miller with his pitch-perfect ear was one of the first American writers to imaginatively explore this world. I thought it was good movie material and optioned the novel. I did not seriously think about directing the movie myself since I was completely inexperienced. I had seen Shirley Clarke's film *The Connection* (1961) and admired it. I contacted Shirley and she agreed to direct and edit the film. I was the producer. The film was released in 1964. The story of the production of *The Cool World* is much too long and torturous to include here. Working on *The Cool World* was both a depressing and liberating experience— depressing because of all the difficulties in financing, making, and distributing the movie, and liberating because my experience working on the production completely demystified the process of filmmaking for me. After *The Cool World*, I wanted to continue to make movies but only those that I directed, produced, and edited myself.

Filmmaking and the Institutional Series

In 1964 I had the idea of making a movie about MCI Bridgewater. The superintendent agreed, and after a year and a half of intermittently intensive lobbying, I was granted permission to make the film. The shooting of the film that became *Titicut Follies* set the pattern of technique and approach for all my films except *La Dernière Lettre* (*The Last Letter*, 2002) which was made in a more traditional fictional film style.

State Legislature. 2006

Many of the early synchronous sound films were about one person. A famous criminal, rock star, or politician, or someone who was all three. My films are about institutions, the place is the star. I have no precise definition of "institution" other than a place that has existed for a while and that has fairly circumscribed geographical boundaries and where the staff is thought to be trying to do a good job. The institution serves the same purpose for me that the lines and net do for a tennis match: it provides boundaries. What takes place inside the boundaries is fit for inclusion in the film. Outside is another film. I had the idea for doing an institutional series while shooting *Titicut Follies*. It seemed a natural progression to go from a prison for the criminally insane to a high school. Since then I have made thirty-six films about institutions. The cumulative effect is to try to provide an impressionistic portrait, obviously incomplete, of some aspects of contemporary American life as reflected through institutions important for the functioning of American society. (There have been four French films, each on a subject that was not possible in America. For example, there is no American theater or ballet company with the continuity, tradition, and history of the Comédie-Française or the ballet company of the Paris Opéra.)

Funding

This is the least interesting aspect. The funding sources have varied. *Titicut Follies* was made possible because DuArt Laboratory in New York extended credit for all the lab work and agreed not to be paid for six years. In gratitude I have used them for all my other films (with one exception) except those shot outside America. The cash needed came from a few loyal friends and active use of my American Express card. For *High School* (1968), the second film, I received a foundation grant that covered half the costs and DuArt and American Express the rest. Starting with *Law and Order* (1969), I began to be partially funded by the Public Broadcasting Service (PBS) and several foundations. From 1971 to 1981 I had a contract with WNET, Channel 13, the public television station in New York, to do one film a year. The funding for this contract came from the Ford Foundation and was earmarked for my use. Fred Friendly, the former head of CBS News, was in charge of the film program at the Ford Foundation, and he liked what I was doing and arranged the grant so that I could continue to work. Since 1981 the money for the films has come from a variety of sources—PBS, the Corporation for Public Broadcasting Independent Television Service, the Ford, MacArthur, and

Diamond foundations, The National Endowment for the Arts, The National Endowment for the Humanities, and occasionally from the BBC or Channel 4 in England and Canal Plus, ARTE, Planète, and the Centre National du Cinéma in France. I can also be seen on Saturday afternoons in Cambridge, Massachusetts, in front of the Harvard Coop singing and offering pencils for sale.

Permission

For most films (except *Titicut Follies*) getting permission has been easy. I ask the person in charge of the institution for permission in a letter which includes the names of the crew and their respective jobs, the filmmaking technique, a list of the types of sequences I would like to shoot (this list is meant to be not definitive but hypothetical, simply a way to give a full sense of the range of activities to which I would like to have access), the approximate duration of the shooting, a description of the editing process, a statement that I retain editorial control, the possible venues where and mediums through which the film will be shown (theaters, television, DVD), and a list and description of my previous films and an offer to make them available. I ask for complete access to everything that is going on in the institution with the understanding that if anyone does not want to be photographed or recorded I will respect their decision, which must be communicated to me before, during, or immediately following any sequence they appear in. I make it clear that neither the administration of the institution nor any of the participants has a right of review after the film is shot or edited. If the head of the institution agrees, I ask that they sign the letter and return it to me. This letter, while not written in legal language, has the legal status of a contract between me and the institution.

Releases

I do not get written consents from the people photographed, but I tape their consents. This is easier for me and is less scary to the participants who may feel they are signing away ownership rights to their houses or cars. When the subject matter is a public institution, i.e., an institution supported with public funds (taxpayers' money), I do not need to get either written or tape-recorded releases. There are a number of United States Supreme Court decisions that hold that whatever may occur in a public institution is news and is protected by the First Amendment to the United States Constitution, which guarantees freedom of speech and press. This issue goes well beyond the narrow interest of the filmmaker to protect himself from suit for invasion of privacy. The First Amendment is a statement by the framers of the Constitution that all the activities of government (with the exception of issues related to national security) should be transparent so that the citizens of a democracy can have the information they need to make informed decisions about their government and those whom they elect to represent them.

Research

For most films I only visit for a day or two before the shooting starts. All I try to do in advance is to get a sense of the physical space where the film will be shot and make preliminary inquiries to discover the various people who control the decision-making. I do not like to do more than that in advance of the shooting. I am always afraid that something really interesting will happen while I am there doing "research" and that I will miss it for the film, which would make me very sad. The shooting of the film is the research.

The Comédie-Française was the only place I spent more than a few days doing "research" in advance of the shooting. The administrator of the Comédie in 1994 was Jean-Pierre Miquel. He immediately gave me permission to make the film but said I needed to have the consent of the cardinals. The reference was not to suggest that he was the pope but only to indicate that there were twenty-three unions at the Comédie and that I would need their permission before I could start. I spent three months informally wandering around the Comédie, meeting the technicians and telling them about the film. The unions then voted to give me permission. During this time I saw many events I would like to have had for the film. This experience confirmed for me the value of my usual approach.

I try to approach the shooting with a clear but empty head, empty at least of any ideological baggage that can be used to provide an explanation of what I am about to observe. It is only during the editing that I discover the themes and structure of the film. I like to think that the edited film is a report on what I have learned rather than the imposition of a preconceived point of view on the experience. If all I am doing is the latter, I see no reason to make the film. I hope that in each film I discover something for myself. It is not important to me that others may already know what I have learned. I did not.

Most of the films have been shot in one building or several adjacent buildings with the exception of *Canal Zone* (1977) and *Manoeuvre* (1979). These two films were shot over a large geographical area. For the films shot in one building or several adjacent buildings I walk around to find out where the executive offices are, get some preliminary sense of the routine (most of the institutions are open twenty-four hours a day, some, like Neiman Marcus, the subject of *The Store* [1983] eight to ten hours a day), ask about the time and place of weekly staff meetings or any regularly scheduled activity, and begin to develop my own network of informants (not in the police sense of the term)—people who work at the place and are willing to talk with me. For example, the first day I was at Northeast High in Philadelphia for *High School* a man introduced himself to me as the Dean of Discipline. I thought this was an intriguing if somewhat ambiguous job title and he suggested that if I wanted to understand his job I should come to his office at 9:15 in the morning and I would find the "culprits" lined up outside his door. Soon after the shooting started I went to his office, which was easy to find given the size of the line. All the students who had violated the rules of the school were there. It was a mini police court and the Dean of Discipline would act as both prosecutor and judge for such offenses as throwing chalk in class, beating up another student, being late for study hall, or locking up another student or sometimes a teacher in a closet. The Dean not only sentenced the student to, for example, a three-day suspension from school or after-school study hall or an apology, but often made a somewhat formal statement of the values of the school that the student had violated. This kind of more "abstract" statement made by a staff member is one of the hardest things to find in shooting the films. It is rare in my experience that people step back and make a formal statement of the values the institution represents or wants to foster or maintain. The Dean's office became difficult to stay away from for this reason and also because the conversations that took place were very funny. For example:

DR. ALLEN (THE DEAN OF DISCIPLINE): Michael, this had to do with your cutting—what is it? Physical Science?

MICHAEL: No, sir. I never cut it. Mrs. Ganin was yelling at me after class and she starts going off. And you see, somehow I was making noise in the lunch line and the truth is, Mr. Allen, I was behaving in the back of the room. I didn't open my mouth 'cause, see, the other kids were, and I didn't feel like goofing off. And she thought it was me. And she calls me up and she starts yelling at me, and I say, "It wasn't me!" and she starts yelling, yelling, wah wah! So I figure, Mr. Allen, could you stand there and listen to a lady yell? I figure I'd go out and talk to her later when she's calmed down. And she was pretty worked up. And I went to walk out and she goes, "You don't leave." And I go, "I'll speak to you later at a better time." And I walked out because—

DR. ALLEN: First of all, Michael, you showed poor judgment. When you're being addressed by someone older than you are or in a seat of authority, it's your job to respect and listen. She didn't ask you to jump from the Empire State Building; she's not asking you for your blood. She's asking for a little bit of time, to help you out. Now here's the thing: what you should have done is showed some character, by saying, "Okay. I will go to your detention, but may I speak with you and get this matter corrected?"

MICHAEL: She didn't assign a detention.

DR. ALLEN: Well, according to this—

MICHAEL: No, they sent me—

DR. ALLEN, *overlapping*: "Given the choice of a detention at 7:30 or at 1:45 and you refused to take either." Now what is it?

MICHAEL: They sent me down to Mr. Walsh and I tried to explain it to him and he started yelling at me too.

DR. ALLEN: Well, no one is going to yell at you and—

MICHAEL: Well, I don't feel I have to take anybody's screaming at me for nothing—

DR. ALLEN: No, well, there's a point to that, but in the meantime it's time you showed a little character on your own, right?

MICHAEL: Yes, sir.

DR. ALLEN: I would take the detention and then you can come back and say, "Now, I took the detention, may I speak with you and get this—"

MICHAEL: I can't, I can't talk to that man—

DR. ALLEN: Well, you can try.

MICHAEL: Do you know, now another time in that class—this is another reason why I won't take it.

DR. ALLEN: Why?

MICHAEL: I was given a . . . These kids took a book

and they were going to throw it at me, right? And the teacher caught him with the book in his hand and he took it off the other kid's book. And the other kid stood up and says, "Give me my damn book back!" So Mrs. Ganin says, "You two get out! You know, I don't want language around here and no use to get uproared." Do you know that they brought me into the detention room? They brought me into Mr. Walsh's room and they got me dragged in for nothing, and I tried to explain it to him and he says, "Will you take your detention?" Which was utterly ridiculous.

DR. ALLEN: Now, see, we are out to establish something, aren't we?

MICHAEL: Yes!

DR. ALLEN: We're out to establish that you can be a man and that you can take orders. We want to prove to them that you can take the orders.

MICHAEL: But, Mr. Allen, you see, it's all against my principles. You have to stand for something!

DR. ALLEN: Yes. But I think your principles aren't involved here. I think it's a question now of . . . of proving yourself to be a man. It's a question here of how . . . how do we follow rules and regulations.

If there's a mistake made, there's an approach to it. I think you don't fight with a teacher; I think you ask permission to talk. And ask them to listen to you. Now, this is what you didn't do. Now if you take your detention—and after all, they didn't require much from you. The teacher felt you were out of order, and in her judgment you deserved a detention. I don't see anything wrong with assigning you a detention. Now I think you should prove yourself. You should show that you can take the detention when given it.

MICHAEL: I should prove that I am a man and that's what I intend to do by doing what I feel, in my opinion, is what I am doing is right.

DR. ALLEN: Are you going to take your detention or aren't you? I feel that you should.

MICHAEL: I'll take it, but under protest.

DR. ALLEN: All right, then. You take it under protest. That's good.

MICHAEL: Today?

DR. ALLEN: Yes, I'd like you to take it today.

MICHAEL: Will today after school be okay?

DR. ALLEN: Okay.

MICHAEL: What room? Room 120?

DR. ALLEN: 118.

MICHAEL: All right.

While the comedy value of this exchange between the Dean of Discipline and the student is important, the sequence also serves as a good example of the way attitudes toward authority are transmitted and enforced. The sequence is valuable in helping to suggest some of the more general ideas about education that the film is trying to reach.

The Crew

The crew consists of three people. I direct, do the sound, and work with a cameraman and an assistant. Almost all the films have been shot by one of two great cameramen, John Davey or William Brayne. Their skills have made a great contribution to the films, and I am extremely grateful for their help, interest, support, and enthusiasm.

Shooting the Film

The approach has not changed much over the years, although I like to think I have learned something from film to film. I start, as I indicated earlier, with no fixed idea of the themes, point of view, or length of the film.

The goal during the shooting is to collect sequences that interest me. I try to find the power centers of the institution and spend a lot of time following people in authority. For example, at the Comédie-Française I was with Jean-Pierre Miquel in his office and attended many committee meetings that he chaired, particularly the Comité d'Administration, which has real power over the appointment of tenured actors. For *Juvenile Court* (1973), many sequences were shot in the judge's chambers and in the courtroom where he presided. For *La Danse—Le Ballet de l'Opéra de Paris* (2009), most of the time was spent shooting rehearsals and performances but many sequences were shot in the office of Brigitte Lefèvre, the director of the company.

I have no fixed conviction about where to go, other than to hang out with the powerful and the powerless. I have learned the value of following my instincts or "hunches." While they are often wrong they are also occasionally right. I am always willing to take the risk of shooting because otherwise I risk missing a good sequence. I have to trust my instinct that an event is worth shooting. This, which might be called the Las Vegas aspect of film-making, is the principal reason it is necessary to shoot a lot of film. To mix the metaphor, I am trying to harvest a crop which I have not planted and which may not exist. Sometimes I may decide to follow someone because I like their hat or they are cross-eyed or I like the way they walk or there is something interesting about the clothes they are wearing. In shooting a meeting it is very important to collect shots of people not talking or get a wide shot of the group sitting around the table. These shots are invaluable in condensing an hour-long meeting to six minutes. I try to get sequences in all or most of the activities that take place at the institution. While all this may seem obvious, it was not always so for me. I think I have learned most about filmmaking from editing, for only in the editing room do I know that I have the right combination of shots from which to construct the film. What I do not have in one film I tend to remember to try and get in the next one. Hopefully this has had a cumulative beneficial effect.

Each day the cameraman and I constantly discuss the best way to shoot the events we are observing and the type of shots that will accurately convey the scene. The talk is leisurely when there is nothing worth shooting, and more intense, with lots of verbal and nonverbal shorthand, during a sequence. One of the advantages of working with the same person over a long period is that we know each other well and can communicate quickly and accurately. Each event has to be shot in a way that there is enough material to make it both comprehensible and, to the extent possible, beautiful to look at. I always make jokes about the films being shot in "wobblyscope," but the effort during the shooting is to avoid this effect and make the shots as aesthetically pleasing as possible. The formal aspects of the shot are of maximum importance to me, and a lot of effort is made to achieve a pleasing result. At the end of each day's shooting we watch silent rushes of the previous day's work, discuss alternative ways of shooting similar situations, and try to anticipate the different kinds of sequences that may occur and how they might be shot. I make notes summarizing the sequences shot and lists of shots that I need. The rushes are then sent back to my editing room, where an assistant synchronizes the sound and the picture.

These rushes are the consequences of choices made. For example, the welfare center where I made *Welfare* (1975) was open to receive clients nine hours a day, five days a week. In a week, one hundred welfare workers, including social workers, clerical staff, and supervisors, may meet twenty-five hundred clients. At a minimum, a client may talk to three staff members and may speak with at least one other client. There will be at least ten thousand conversations of one sort or another per week and sixty thousand over the six weeks of the shoot. This is a conservative estimate. The actual number is probably much greater. From these sixty thousand encounters I make a selection of what to shoot. A reasonable estimate might be three thousand from the potential sixty thousand, or about five percent of the possible exchanges. Each of the events shot can be filmed in a variety of ways, i.e., wide shot, medium shot, and close up, with all the possibilities that exist in each of these categories, which of course include changes of angle and position. I am not a mathematician and hesitate to say that there are an infinite number of possible choices. This is just speculation since I am only aware theoretically that all these choices exist, but for each film there are certainly a lot of possibilities.

The time of the shooting of the film varies. *Titicut Follies, High School*, and *Welfare* were each shot in four weeks, *Basic Training* (1971) in nine weeks, *La Comédie-Française* (1996) and *La Danse* in twelve weeks. The shooting of performance films is longer because of the need to include both rehearsal and performance. Generally, the length of the shooting varies according to the subject matter, the nature of the activities, my interest, and the quality of the hotel accommodations.

Editing

I like to edit my films. There is something very satisfying for me in trying to find a form for my experience or at least that part of my experience that working on a movie represents.

In the editing a different series of choices emerges. The rushes are the physical manifestation of the choices made in the shooting. The rushes, this great glop of material which represents the record of my experience of the time I was present at the institution, are obviously only the external, material form of the experience and are, of course, incomplete. The memories not preserved on film float somewhere in my mind as fragments available for recall, unavailable for inclusion but of great importance in the mining and sifting process called editing. This editorial process, which is sometimes deductive, sometimes associational, sometimes non-logical, and sometimes a failure, is occasionally boring but most often exciting. The crucial aspect for me is to try to think through my own relationship to the material by whatever combination of means occurs to and works for me. This results in a four-way conversation between myself, the sequence being worked on, my memory, and some consciousness of my values and alertness to my experience.

Most of the sequences are too long to use as shot. In fact, most of them are not used. My first task as editor is to evaluate the sequences from the shoot. There are many ways of doing this. I use a classification system adapted from the Michelin Guide—one, two, or three stars. (The use of forks and spoons would only complicate matters.) This first pass at the material usually results in the rejection of at least fifty percent of the rushes. I then have a list of candidate sequences for possible inclusion in the film. Over a period of six to eight months I edit these sequences into what I consider a usable form. A sequence as it occurred in what can be called "real time" may last an hour. Of that hour fifty-eight minutes is shot. I then edit the fifty-eight minutes to eight minutes. The eight minutes selected might be eight consecutive minutes but it is more likely to be eight minutes selected from different parts of the original fifty-eight: forty-five seconds here, thirty seconds there, two minutes here, fifteen seconds there, until a sequence is created that resembles but is not the original, yet is a fair representation. Within a

sequence I never change the order of the events. The edited version has to appear as if it took place the way the viewer is seeing it, when, of course, it did not. In this sense the edited sequence is a "fiction," because, if it works, it creates the illusion, however momentary, that the scene originally occurred in the form used in the final film. One aspect of the editing is to confirm or reject the original choice to shoot the sequence and to convey an interpretation of the selected event in a comprehensible, condensed form. Also, some sequences, usually short, are used as they were originally photographed and recorded.

When I am evaluating and editing a sequence I have to ask myself questions that have nothing to do with the technical aspects of filmmaking. This part of the editing has more to do with an analysis of behavior. I have to constantly ask myself the following kinds of questions: Why are the participants saying what they are saying? What are the implications of the choice of words spoken or not spoken? What is the significance of a gesture, a tone or change of tone, a look, a walk? What inferences, if any, can be made from choice of clothes? I do not know if I am right about the inferences I make, but I have to have a theory about what is occurring in order to make the choices as to whether I want to use the sequence, how I am going to edit it, and finally if and where I might place it in the film.

All sequences are examples of the variety of distortions which have their origin in the differences between the mechanical apparatuses of camera and tape recorder and the human eye, ear, and mind.

It takes me six to eight months to edit into a usable form all the sequences that are candidates for inclusion in the final film. Only then can I begin work on the structure. I am not able to work on the structure in the abstract. I have to see and hear how the sequences go together. There is a lot of trial and error in this, but because the sequences are already edited it is possible to try, very quickly, different ways of organizing the material. Frequently, the order in which the sequences are arranged has little or no relation to the order in which they were shot. I might begin the film with a shot from the thirtieth day of shooting and end with a sequence from the third day. However, I never change the order of events within a sequence. At this point, around the eighth month of editing, everything is "material" and has to be arranged in an order which best presents the themes, ideas, and characterizations I find in the rushes. A principal part of my job as editor is to try to think through the meaning of the sequences individually and then the implications of arranging them in a particular order that works as a dramatic structure. There is some similarity between the work of imagining and choosing the structure and fiction-writing, whether for a novel, play, poem, or screenplay. The film structure is invented or imagined within the limitations imposed by the original rushes and their possible combinations in an edited form. Even with this limitation a great variety of structures are possible but obviously not as many as in a traditional work of fiction where there is a different ratio of experience to imagination. I usually can make the first assembly of the film in three or four days, after eight months of working with the material, because at that point I know the material very well and can recite all the dialogue and recall all the images. The first assembly usually is thirty to forty minutes longer than the final film. I then need four to six weeks to arrive at the final film. Most of this time is spent working on the rhythm of the film—the internal rhythm within a sequence and the external rhythm of the shots that link or are the transition between major sequences. To arrive at the right rhythm I have to experiment to find out how the sound and the picture best work together.

I do not add narration or music. There is a lot of music in the films but it is all music recorded during the filming as it occurs. I do not like to use narration or ask questions of the participants. When a sequence in one of my films "works," I think it is because the viewers feel physically, intellectually, and emotionally present and can make up their own minds about what they are seeing and hearing. It is my job to provide enough information so this can happen. A narrator or an interviewer is an obstacle to this effort of immediate involvement.

When I think the editing is close to being finished I look at all the rushes I originally rejected, usually fifty to sixty hours of material. I often find shots or sequences that I had originally rejected very useful for solving an editorial problem. It may be something as simple as a shot of a man walking down a corridor that may be a better transition than the shot I used or that can be placed where a transition had not previously existed but was necessary. Sometimes I find shots that help in the characterization of someone important in the film or that make more comprehensible a sequence that had been obscure. Finally, I have to be able to go through the film sequence by sequence and explain to myself why each shot was used, the reason for its particular placement and the relationship of all the sequences to each other. For example, I have to understand the connection between the first and last minutes of the film and the significance of the order selected for the intervening sequences. The film has to work for me on a literal level and at its periphery as a metaphor or at least an abstract statement that is more than the sum of the literal meaning of each sequence. While there is no way of my knowing what influenced me, I like to think that the greatest influence on my editing of the films has been the attention to close reading I was taught in college and the novels and poems I have since tried to read with care.

In a film of three hours only three percent of the original hundred hours of rushes is used. If only five percent of the possible material is included in the rushes and only three percent of that five percent is used, then only fifteen ten-thousandths of the possible original choice of sequences make it into the final film. The films vary greatly in length, the shortest lasting one hour, the longest six hours. The length is determined by the complexity of the material and the necessity of being fair to the participants.

When the editorial process is finished the film exists in its final form. Assuming the film "works" as a

Law and Order. 1969

dramatic structure, the result may be a reflection of a reality, an interpretation of a reality, a new reality, or none of the above. The real reality of the film may exist only at the unidentifiable point where the eye, ear, and mind of the viewer meet the screen.

The Camera and Behavior

Does the camera change behavior? There is no definitive answer to that question other than maybe, sometimes, but for the most part no. In my experience most people are not good enough actors to suddenly change their behavior because their picture is being taken and their voice recorded. If they were, then the pool of potential actors for the stage or movies would be much larger than it already is. If someone does not want to be in the film, he will say "no," walk away, or thumb his nose. Like anyone who meets many people, I have had to try to develop a good bullshit meter in order to survive. I have to make a quick judgment as to whether or not I am being conned, i.e., whether the people being photographed are acting for the camera or saying or doing things they would not say or do if they were not being photographed or recorded. There has been an enormous variety of human behavior recorded in all the documen-

tary films ever made. It is probably safe to say that not all the possible combinations of words, gestures, and acts are on film but certainly a staggeringly large number are. If the camera generally affected behavior, one assumption might be that it pushed people toward a bland center where their acts would not be noticed. Also, if being photographed changed behavior, the manufacturers of film equipment would replace doctors and pharmacologists as agents of change.

In my experience people act in ways they think are appropriate for the situation they are in without regard to the presence of the camera and tape recorder. An example. In 1968 I shot *Law and Order*, a film about the police department in Kansas City, Missouri. In Kansas City at the time, in order to make an arrest for prostitution, the police had to have a price and an act. An undercover policeman would pick up a woman and go back to a hotel with her. The policeman had to negotiate a price, get undressed, and presumably at the last minute make the arrest. We were in the vice squad car one night when a call came in from an undercover policeman that a woman had assaulted him and fled after he had arrested her. The vice squad car immediately went to the seedy hotel where this had taken place. The undercover policeman met us in the lobby and reported that as he was leading the woman from the first-floor room she had broken away from him, knocked him down the stairs. The bellboy said the woman had run to the basement. The basement was very dark. By chance we had a sun gun (a very powerful light used for filming when there is no natural light or not enough artificial light). The police found the woman in a basement room hiding under some broken and discarded furniture. The sun gun was on so that we could film the sequence. When the woman was dragged out, one of the policeman put his arm around her neck and started to choke her. The woman began to make gurgling noises, and after fifteen or twenty seconds he let her go. As he let her go, the woman turned to another policeman who was holding her arms and said, referring to the first policeman, "He was choking me." To which the second policeman replied, "Nobody was choking you, you're imagining it." All of this is on film. I do not believe that the police would have killed the woman had we not been there. The woman had been working as a prostitute for only a few weeks and the police were initiating her. They were telling her that if she wanted to be a prostitute that was okay but that there were limits to her behavior. One rule she had to learn was not to disobey the police. If she got arrested, she had to go along with it and pay the fine and then could be back out on the street in an hour. If she did not play along, she would be treated roughly. The policeman had no problem choking the woman in front of the camera and tape recorder because he did not see anything wrong with his behavior. This is the way you treat a prostitute who attacks a policeman. She was being taught a lesson. The lesson for me, the filmmaker, in this story is that most of us, most of the time, act in ways we think are appropriate, but others may not agree with our self-evaluation. The policeman thought it was all right to choke the woman. His colleagues agreed. Most of us watching the sequence do not agree. It could be filmed because the police thought they were acting appropriately, as most of us do most of the time, even though others may not agree. This is my case for the camera not changing behavior and therefore being a small exception to the Heisenberg principle.

Distribution

My films are distributed by Zipporah Films in Cambridge, Massachusetts, a company that I set up in 1971 because

I had been cheated by professional distributors who made money with my films but were not interested in giving any back to me. It was a very easy decision to make since I had nothing to lose. The mistakes would be mine and any income that came in I could keep. The distribution company and my office have been run for thirty years by Karen Konicek. Her intelligence, loyalty, and good humor in arranging the distribution of my films and in dealing with the vagaries of my life have made it possible for me to continue to make movies.

All of my films have been shown on public television (PBS) in America, on ARTE and Planète in France, on RAI in Italy, and on Planète in Spain and Germany. Many have been broadcast in England on either the BBC or Channel 4. Some have also been shown on television in many other countries. The films have had limited theatrical distribution in the United States. *La Danse* is the only film that has had a wide theatrical distribution in many countries. The other films have had a very limited theatrical showing. All of the films are available on DVD.

Theater

Apart from my private theater at home, my parents took me to see plays acknowledged as professional productions. When I was young I saw many musical comedies. In my adolescence I saw whatever touring companies passed through Boston and attended productions of *Henry V*, *Hamlet*, and *Othello*. In law school I occasionally disappeared to New York for a week here and there to go the theater. In Paris from 1956 to 1958, I was able to see plays by Anouilh, Ionesco, Sartre, and Pirandello. There were marvelous productions of Molière at the Comédie-Française with Robert Hirsch, Louis Seigner, Jacques Charon, and Robert Manuel. I saw Peter Brook's production of *Titus Andronicus* with Laurence Olivier, Anthony Quayle, Vivien Leigh, and Maxine Audley. I went to the theater at least three times a week.

In the 1960s and '70s I was often in London and was a regular at the Royal Shakespeare Company there and in Stratford-upon-Avon and later frequently attended the National Theatre. One time at Stratford I saw Alan Howard appear in *Henry IV*, parts one and two, *Henry V*, and *Coriolanus* in consecutive performances in three days. I still go to the theater a lot, certainly as much as the movies.

In 1986 I was asked by Robert Brustein, the director of the American Repertory Theater in Cambridge, to participate in a production of *Tonight We Improvise*

La Dernière Lettre (*The Last Letter*). 2002

by Luigi Pirandello. I suggested, with the posthumous approval of Pirandello, that I add the character of a documentary filmmaker making a movie about the production. I was on stage and shot the play as it was being acted. The audience thus had the choice of watching the actors or the rushes of the actors projected on a twelve-by-twelve-foot screen. Halfway through the play I also presented a narrated documentary about Sicily that was done in an opposite style to my films. This was my first experience on the stage and working with actors. It was a considerable contrast to the solitude of the editing room. I enjoyed the experience.

I wanted to work more in the theater. In 1988 at the American Repertory Theater I first directed *The Last Letter*, an adaptation I had done of a chapter from Vasily Grossman's great novel *Life and Fate* (1959). The novel takes place in the Soviet Union from 1918 through the battle of Stalingrad. *Life and Fate* is in the grand tradition of Tolstoy, Dostoyevsky, and Babel. The chapter that I adapted is a letter a Russian Jewish doctor writes to her son a few nights before she knows she will be killed by the Germans, who have occupied her village in the Ukraine. The letter is a recapitulation of her life, written with the hope that it will reach her son, a

Russian physicist safely working in a physics institute on the Soviet atomic bomb. I had discovered the Grossman text in Paris when two French actors read it in a little theater in Montparnasse. In 2000 I had a chance to direct the *The Last Letter*, as *La Derniére Lettre,* at the Comédie-Française. Jean-Pierre Miquel, the administrator of the Comédie-Française, had liked my film about the Comédie and asked if I wanted to direct a play there. I took about a nanosecond to say yes and I suggested *The Last Letter*. Jean-Pierre Miquel read and liked the play and agreed.

I had met Catherine Samie before I started working on the film about the Comédie-Française. She then was doyenne (the senior actor) of the Comédie and her approval for making the film was necessary. Catherine and I got along well and she was very helpful during the shooting, suggesting many events that were important for the film. I thought Catherine would be perfect for the part of the mother in *La Dernière Lettre*. She read the script and immediately agreed. We spent ten weeks rehearsing and the play was performed at the Studio-Théâtre at the Comédie-Française and toured in France, the United States, and Canada. Catherine is a great actress and her performance in *La Dernière Lettre* was brilliant. She gave a full characterization of a woman who was intelligent, charming, flirtatious, and difficult, a successful doctor and a loving but demanding mother. While I may be prejudiced, it was one of the finest performances I have ever seen. In 2002 I made a film of *La Dernière Lettre* with Catherine.

I also directed *The Last Letter* in New York for Theatre for a New Audience with the American actress Kathleen Chalfant, who was also brilliant in the part.

I wanted to do another play and talked to Jean-Pierre Miquel and his successor, Marcel Bozonnet, about doing Samuel Beckett's *Oh les beaux jours* (*Happy Days*) with Catherine playing Winnie and Yves Gasc, another senior actor at the Comédie, as Willie. I love Beckett's work and I felt privileged to have the good luck to direct this cosmicomic, sad masterpiece in 2005–06. The play was a lot of hard work for all of us. Beckett is very precise in his stage directions and at the same time it was important for us to find a way of presenting the play that was consistent with our understanding of Winnie and Willie. My work in films helped. In making the films I had come across a wide variety of people in tragic, sad, and funny situations. I was able to use my memory of those film experiences both in understanding Beckett's play and as a stimulus for making suggestions to Catherine

and Yves. For example, in making *Domestic Violence* (2001) I had met many women whose relationships are well described by the cliché "dysfunctional." In *Oh les beaux jours* it is important to understand the literal aspect of Willie and Winnie being a couple, and to use this as a base from which to reach the more abstract aspects of the play. I was able to use the experience in one form, film, to help me work with actors creating characters based on written words that would then be brought to life in another form, a staged play. Catherine was brilliant as Winnie, showing the sad, funny, and complaisant aspects of her character. Yves Gasc was superb as Willie, a small but demanding role. Willie is the provocateur for Winnie's monologues. The play was brought back later in 2006 and Yves Gasc was not available to play Willie and Muriel Mayette, the new administrator of the Comédie, asked me to play Willie. I felt very privileged to have my stage debut at the Comédie-Française. No one has yet asked me to play Lear.

Conclusion

This is a brief over- or underview of my career. I have had a good time, a lot of laughs, and an intense, concentrated professional life. For me, there is no better way to pass the time. It certainly beats working for a living.

1. Lewis Carroll, *Alice's Adventures in Wonderland* (London: Penguin Books, 1998), pp. 40–41.

La Danse—Le Ballet de l'Opéra de Paris. 2009

Manoeuvre. 1979

Imagination Alive Imagine

Christopher Ricks

New Year's Day, 2010. And Twenty Ten rang at once to the strains of "Happy Birthday," welcoming Frederick Wiseman to being eighty. His vision is still twenty-twenty, 20/20. The Snellen fraction was devised to calculate the particular power in which Wiseman excels: visual acuity.

Sigmund Freud wrote to his more-than-disciple Ernest Jones in 1936,

> What is the secret meaning of this celebrating the big round numbers of one's life? Surely a measure of triumph over the transitoriness of life, which, as we never forget, is ready to devour us. Then one rejoices with a sort of communal feeling that we are not made of such frail stuff as to prevent one of us victoriously resisting the hostile effects of life for sixty, seventy or even eighty years.

Celebrating is the *mot juste*, especially here and now in our all seeking to do justice to the big rounded life that Wiseman has long led, his art—like all art—itself constituting a measure of triumph over the transitoriness of life. This, with the word "measure" meaning not just a certain amount, as when we speak of a measure of success, but a true way of measuring. (Is man the measure of all things?) For triumph can be and should be precisely measured. Art celebrates, though it does not do only this, and Wiseman's films—like countless moments within them—are celebratory, even when on occasion all that can honorably be celebrated turns out to be someone's heartening resistance to everything that is dishonorable, degrading, callous, or specious. Art does rejoice (to stay with another of Freud's words), though again it does not do only this, and Wiseman's films make manifest both how much and how little cause we have to rejoice in this life. In the words of another artist of genius,

> Consequently I rejoice, having to construct something
> Upon which to rejoice

> —T. S. Eliot, *Ash-Wednesday*, 1930

Wiseman, like Eliot, not only constructs but construes, as any true artist does. Wiseman, too, is duly wary as to this whole matter of rejoicing, setting himself to construct works that understand the difference between something *in* which, *about* which, or *at* which to rejoice, as against something *upon* which to rejoice. To turn back again to Freud's words, while it is true that all art—like those big round numbers of one's life—must depend upon "a sort of communal feeling," the art of film accords a particular place to communal feeling, and the art of documentary film accords a further particular place to all such communal feelings as go to the making of communities—such communities as institutions, for instance a school, a hospital, a store, a court, a park, a zoo, these being the realities that Wiseman knows best, in the sense not only of knowing them even better than he knows other things but of knowing them better than anyone else does. As for some "measure of triumph over the transitoriness of life," and "resisting the hostile effects of life" (that is to say, the effects of death, when you think about it), we did not need Freud to remind us—though it does help—that there are three ways in which mankind sets itself to achieve a measure of triumph.

These are three ancient and universal forms of afterlife that many yearn for and some pray for: the afterlife of religious faith; that of children, and of the children of the children of one's child; and that of artistic accomplishment. For Wiseman as an artist, it is this last of the trinity that has to be the consummation devoutly to be wished. The foundation for his achievement is that his art not only creates an afterlife for itself but contemplates with remarkable imaginative intensity all three of the sovereign ways in which some such measure of triumph may be glimpsed. Only one of the films can bear the title *Near Death*, but there is a sense in which the title of this particular masterpiece—alive through six hours of many pangs and of skilled compassion—might offer itself as the subtitle of all of Wiseman's masterpieces: near death, as a subtitle six feet under. Or, as literary theory might be pleased to purr, *under erasure*. But then the great erasure is death; we are always near death, given that in the midst of life we are in death, and that to stay alive must for each of us more and more come to mean nearing death. So says a septuagenarian who is here celebrating an octogenarian. Philip Larkin is one of the many writers who capture the imagination of Wiseman the imaginer (Samuel Beckett being the greatest of these, as was clear from Wiseman's Paris production of *Oh les beaux jours* in 2005–06), and Larkin has many an arrowy memento mori in his quiver. "Most things may never happen: this one will." Or, bringing to an end another poem, "And age, and then the only end of age."

Think of how, and how much, and where, and why, Wiseman's films range so. Religious faith first and (for those who possess it) foremost. This has been one of the films' constants, itself understood as constituting a constant for anyone with faith. It is actively present—is presented in action and in convincingly various forms—in films from *Titicut Follies* (1967) through *Hospital, Basic Training, Juvenile Court, Welfare, Canal Zone, Sinai Field Mission, Manoeuvre, Blind, Deaf, Missile, Central Park, Near Death, Aspen, Public Housing, Belfast, Maine*, and *Domestic Violence* through to *State Legislature* (2006), and including Wiseman's adaptation of Vasily Grossman's novel *Life and Fate* (1959), the tragedy from the Holocaust that is *La Dernière Lettre* (2002).

A seeing of life under the aspect of religious faith is everywhere in the films and in their filming. Added to which, there is one film that contemplates directly not only the religious life but the life of *a religious* (in the ancient sense of one bound by monastic vows or devoted to a religious life according to Catholic principles): *Essene* (1972), shot in a Benedictine monastery, where the daily round, the common task, will furnish all we ought to ask—room to deny ourselves. Or will it? Undeniably the fervor of the believers has its high, thrilling memorability, and then so does a sudden moment of something quite other, with a contiguity of comedy and petty violence such as is respectfully savored on our behalf. Suddenly a priestly figure, more Christian than christian in the comments he relishes making about his Superior at the monastery, whips open a drawer, seizes a flyswatter, swats an errant fly, and swipes shut the drawer. All in a trice. The film as a whole may often show the continuing life within the monastery as though traveling serenely across a tapestry, but this moment of exultant savagery is etched. I can now never hear applied to a Wiseman film the commonplace sappy phrase about "a fly on the wall" without mourning this poor fly, which was not granted even the untrustworthy safety of a wall. Whereupon, in the way that Wiseman's films have of encouraging you to let your mind and your feelings ripple outward, I summon—not without religious feelings for an atheist—the age-old tradition that salutarily, chasteningly, sees man himself as a fly.

Little fly,
Thy summer play
My thoughtless hand
Hath brushed away.

Am not I
A fly like thee
Or art not thou
A man like me?

—William Blake, Songs of Innocence and Experience, 1794

But in the moment that is the essence of *Essene*, the priestly hand was by no means thoughtless, it had one thought and one thought only, which was not exactly— or was exactly not—that of *brushing* the fly away. Thanks to Wiseman, we are led to see another memento mori, a traditional humbling of man's pride (but not this pious man's pride), all of it abruptly compacted in the corporeal vividness of a Charlie Chaplincy. Elsewhere, in the filmed institutions that house the dying, the chaplains come across as sometimes benign, sometimes vulturine.

If, as Robert Frost believed or hoped, poetry is "a momentary stay against confusion," poetry—like any art—aspires to being more than momentary in itself; that is, to *stay* more than momentarily, to endure so as to be of service in the moments of others, now and in the future. A momentary, and even perhaps more than momentary, *stay* against the confusion that is death may be supplied, we can never be too often reminded, by religious faith. Or it may be supplied, in some measure, by the second figure of the trinity, a son or daughter to live in a world of time beyond us. The tender turn is Eliot's, from "Marina" (1930), a poem in which is imagined the hushed meeting of a father, Shakespeare's Pericles, with the daughter whom he has never known:

This form, this face, this life
Living to live in a world of time beyond me; let me
Resign my life for this life.

Time beyond oneself, in the hopes that go to the making of a family with its life that is not only new but opens a vista of life renewing yet again: whether "an ordinary sorrow of man's life" or (in a different phrase from Wordsworth) a "joy in widest commonalty spread," these hopes, anxieties, and disappointments everywhere figure within the compelling sequence of Wiseman's films, from *High School* (1968), through *Law and Order*,

Hospital, Basic Training, Essene, Juvenile Court, Welfare,
Canal Zone, The Store, Blind, Deaf, Multi-handicapped,
Central Park, Near Death, Aspen, Zoo, High School II,
Public Housing, Belfast, Maine, Domestic Violence, and
Domestic Violence 2 through to *State Legislature* (2006).

Does this list establish for Wiseman's art an exact parallel with the other list, that of the other aspiration with which we resist death: religious faith? No, because this time there is no counterpart to the place of *Essene* and religious faith within the body of the films, for there is no one film that takes as its direct object and subject of attention the new and renewing life that is family, understood not only as what we tellingly call *immediate* family but as all the vistas of *mediate* family, the future times that will not be one's own and yet are time laid up in store, there in the dual sense of the one word *generation*. In the first of his publications as poet laureate in 1851, Alfred Tennyson gave loyal voice to his high hopes of Queen Victoria, hopes shared by all art including his own:

> May children of our children say,
> "She wrought her people lasting good"

There being no Wiseman film called *Family* is far from an inadvertence or his not yet happening to have undertaken it. Could it possibly be, then, that to this profound comprehender of institutions the family is not an there being such a film as Wiseman's conscience and consciousness exist to create. The essential privacy of the family deprives Wiseman of an opportunity—and a good thing too, this is not in fact a privation, since he never respected his art more than when he implicitly acknowledged that an abnegation, even a sacrifice, was called for here, that something had to be not just eschewed but waived. Contrast the conscienceless exploitation that is reality television, where a series of cooperating witnesses to family intimacies and humiliations are paid to make an exhibition of themselves and of one another, paid not only down in cash but more crucially in celebrity, the whole thing being our world's squalid version of a gladiator contest, the drab arena for such deaths of the spirit being a living room. I gather that the technical term for this particular art form is a fuckumentary. No problem. For Wiseman, there is no problem either, yet for the opposite reason: his principled abstention from invasion. From the start, back with *Titicut Follies,* his films have raised the question of whether they constitute an invasion of privacy, but as I put it in a tribute to his art twenty years ago (when I adduced twenty-one films in twenty-one years, whereas by now it is nearing a magnificent forty), what it means to speak of an invasion of privacy is often misunderstood. The invasion is not so crucially that of the privacy of those within the very various institutions Wiseman explores as it is that of *our* privacy, our understandable unlovely wish not to have publicly pressed upon us the usually hidden realities of institutional life. Family feelings and thinkings, in all their range and depth, are not the subject of any one film of Wiseman's because they are the element within which the films live, and move, and have their being.

All of which leaves the last member of the trinity of death-tamers: the creation of art. It is upon the creation of art that Wiseman's films have more and more concentrated and rejoiced with the years, and in particular of the performing arts, the nature of which has given him further opportunities for both the extensive and the intensive.

Yet there at the beginning, in 1967, there was *Titicut Follies*, the first film and the one that has as both its first shot and its parting shot a performance of the annual song-and-dance show for the inmates at the state hospital for the criminally insane in Bridgewater, Massachusetts. There is a sense, then, in which (as is the case with Beckett, too) everything was always there from the beginning. But the strength of Wiseman's grasp is his understanding that in all such concepts it is essential to avoid the two equal and opposite dangers, that of defining the concept so rigidly that it dries into petrifaction, and that of defining it so laxly that it sogs into putrefaction. The danger of excluding too much, versus that of including too much.

Under the one head, we need to value the sheer usefulness of a concept of performance that works straightforwardly to help us identify a world of the arts and of culture within the larger world. In this valuably ordinary sense, it was not until *Ballet* in 1995, his film on a classical dance company (the American Ballet Theatre), that Wiseman turned directly to giving central salience to performance. "The language of film is universal": this is the sonorously suspect assurance pronounced to accompany the previews in many an arty cinema, compounded by the repetition of this half-truth in many tongues, some advertisory babble from Babel. Is the language of ballet international? Yes and no. Certainly the American Ballet Theatre is American, but the film itself proceeds to go on tour, from rehearsing in its New York studio to performing in Athens and in Copenhagen. Then how deftly does the term *corps de ballet* make for France. Since 1995 there have been three performance-films: *La Comédie-Française ou l'amour joué* (1996), *La Dernière Lettre*, and *La Danse—Le Ballet de l'Opéra de Paris* (2009).[1]

Not that *Ballet* had been without harbingers, for in 1980 there had been *Model*, one of Wiseman's most exquisite and most saddening films, acute in its sympathy for what it is for a man or a woman to have to stake so much on looking lovely (even when the takes are mounting to take 70-times-7). The people at the heart of *Model* are in many crucial respects not actors, but acting is what is required of them. They give themselves to being filmed, refilmed, and re-refilmed, and none of this in the first instance by Wiseman. Likewise, though as the other side of the coin, the films since *Ballet* and its immediate successor, *La Comédie-Française*, have by no means turned solely to public performance. *La Comédie-Française* was followed by *Public Housing* (1997), after which came films that likewise are not of the performing world: *Belfast, Maine* (1999), *Domestic Violence* (two films, 2001 and 2002), and *State Legislature*. A further film spans any such division, for rather as *Model*

Ballet. 1995

in 1980 had been a straddler (most elegant straddling, in its case), so too is the film of 2004 on Madison Square Garden, *the* Garden: *The Garden*.

But we would exclude too much if we were to limit our notion of performance to such cases—to ballet, to theater, or to film, come to that. For every single one of Wiseman's films has some strong moment or feature that asks to be seen under the aspect of performance. The squirmingly jokey speech on sex education in *High School*, with twenty-six years later the how-to-fit-a-condom demonstration in *High School II*; *Basic Training* rightly seen as finding the basis of any such training in the stylized projecting of authority (Atten-*shun*!); the high-sheen sermon in *Essene*; the courtroom drama that is itself to be judged in *Juvenile Court*, stuck inside of

Memphis, and thirty years later in *Domestic Violence 2*, set in the arraignment, misdemeanor, and injunction courts in Tampa, Florida; the baroque tirade from a down-but-not-out in *Welfare* who out-Becketts Beckett; the rich sales-pitch (to touch it is to be defiled) in *The Store*; the jockeying and not just for position in *Racetrack*; the touching eloquence and dexterous beauty of sign-language not only in the hands but in the full-bodied people in *Deaf*; the skating and the parading in *Central Park*; the performing elephants and their performing trainer in *Zoo*; and the tricksters, hucksters, hustlers, and shysters (with the occasional soothsayer or even truthteller) in *State Legislature*, which has its sudden superb intervention when an electronically controlled toylet scuttles across the floor: all of these are performances of a kind, or rather of a great many kinds, and this without our having at all to stretch the concept of performance beyond its proper bounds. All the world's a stage, and all the men and women merely players. Agreed, provided that to this truth, and in no way to its detriment, we add a further one: that even if all the world's a stage and all the men and women merely players, we are not out of our minds when we purchase a ticket for the theater, since *La Comédie-Française* shows us, you know, a *stage*, and we the audience, unlike those on stage, are in a pretty important respect not actually *players*.

The greatness of Wiseman's art is its so balancing the true claims of both parties to the conversation. There is a sense in which everything may be seen under the aspect of performance, and another equally commonsense sense in which there is a perfectly simple indispensable distinction between performance and other things in life. Of either of the extreme positions it should be believed (in words that are crucially different heard in *King Lear* as against in conversation), "That way madness lies."

One way of measuring Wiseman's wisdom in this whole matter of performance would be to say that his art realizes (in both senses) the truth of Erving Goffman's argument of 1959 that every day and in every way, each of us goes in for role-playing, or for "the presentation of self in everyday life." Such is the show that really must go on. But there is a but, and Wiseman appreciates that Goffman's truth is not the truth, the whole truth, and nothing but the truth. (Nothing ever is, except as a legal fiction.) Goffman, a sociologist who writes so well that one thinks of him as an anthropologist, has a sharp eye for just those ordinary performings for which Wiseman has a sharp lens. Such as this exchange at an airport, when a man neither silently puts down his bag en route to the ticket counter nor explicitly asks the woman sitting there to watch the bag for him. Instead:

> HE [*laconically, almost sotto voce, as if already lodged in conversation with the recipient*]: Don't let them steal it.
>
> SHE [*immediately utters an appreciative conspiratorial chuckle as speaker continues on his way*].

Goffman is rightly confident in such a case, but the overconfidence that can overtake him was clear at a moment when (as it happens) he was watching a film that was being edited: *Titicut Follies*. Goffman's folly was to interrupt the editing at the moment when a Bridgewater inmate is having his face, his eyes, attended to by the prison staff; to remark to Wiseman, pompously, the filmmaker remembers, that the staff are behaving with characteristic dehumanizing coldness; and not to see what was before his eyes, that the inmate is dead and that his face, his eyes, are being restored to some final dignity.

Thanks to Goffman, the last half-century has improved its understanding of social performings. Thanks to Wiseman, it has improved its understanding of the limits of any such understanding. This, because Wiseman's art is concerned to do justice not only to social performance but to the performing arts, justice that can be done only if we hold to a conviction that although there is indeed performing wherever we look, it remains the case that in the theater or at the ballet, what we are watching is a *performance*. Wiseman's latest film, *Boxing Gym* (2010), is superb in the surety with which it brings its many kinds of daily performance (by teacher and taught, spouses and children, braggart and listener) into relation with those performances in the ring. So light on their feet are the boxers, weaving in so seemly and firm a manner, seldom seen sparring much, that *Boxing Gym* at times seems to breathe the air of its immediate predecessor, intimating that we are attending upon *La Danse Revisitée*. A patient passion for *rehearsal* braces and embraces all of these performance-films. Wiseman rightly reveres this passion in the company that he keeps (keeps for us to see), and if it weren't that we already have a play called *The Rehearsal*, from the seventeenth-century days when the Comédie-Française was founded, there would be a case for Wiseman's laying claim to the title. Or at least thinking of it as the unuttered sub-title to *Ballet*, *La Comédie-Française*, *La Dernière Lettre*, *La Danse*, and, yes, *Boxing Gym*.

For this turning to performance-films there was again a harbinger: Wiseman's directing the video sequences, and his acting in the role of a documentary filmmaker, in the 1986 production of Pirandello, *Tonight We Improvise*, at the American Repertory Theater in Cambridge, Massachusetts. There followed in 1988 the first of the theater productions of his adaptation from Grossman, as *The Last Letter*, which was then, in 2000—as *La Dernière Lettre*—restaged at the Comédie-Française and on tour (becoming a film in 2002). His production of Beckett's *Oh les beaux jours* was at the Comédie-Française in 2005–06.

These experiences in and with theater clearly vivify, as one would expect, the performance-films. But what might it be that has drawn Wiseman into giving a new salience to the performing arts? The opportunity, I suggest, to deepen and widen one form in which imagination itself is made manifest. There is a parallel here with the range of what we take to be performance. For just as performing may be the valuably ordinary thing that in some sense we do all the time, so may be imagining,

exercising our imagination. Understood under this aspect, every single film of Wiseman's pays tribute to human powers of imagination and their extraordinary variety, even while needing on occasion to warn us against what Dr. Johnson called the hunger of the imagination that preys upon life. For the sadist is characterized by imagination, and so is the man or woman in the grip of fantasies, paranoia, gullibility. Imagination, in its uses and abuses, is everywhere in Wiseman's films since it is everywhere in life. But at the same time, even as there are not only daily performings but performances of Racine, so, even while all human beings are imaginers, there are some people with a genius for imagining. It is these people, and their sibling genius, to which these recent films of Wiseman's attend, with renewed revelatory power. Actors, dancers, great imaginers, are filmed by a great imaginer who is also a great straight recorder.

John Keats, like many great poets, revered the greatness of others, some of them poets. When he praised John Milton, he said that "one of the most mysterious of semi-speculations is, one would suppose, that of one Mind's imagining into another." Elsewhere, delighting in *The Arabian Nights*, he used the phrase "we imagine after them." It was in this spirit that he evoked the genius of

Edmund Kean as an actor, this time offering as the preposition to follow his intransitive use of the verb to imagine (the transitive does not of course need a preposition) neither *into* nor *after* but *to*, with Kean imagining what the character he was playing was and was not imagining: "In the hypocritical self-possession, in the caution, and afterwards the pride, cruelty, and avarice, Luke appears to us a man incapable of imagining to the extreme heinousness of crimes." And of Kean's Shakespearean acting as continuous with Shakespeare's own imaginative powers Keats wrote, "There is an indescribable gusto in his voice, by which we feel that the utterer is thinking of the past and the future, while speaking of the instant." *Imagining into imaginations*, then. Which is why in the brilliance and poignancy with which Keats's poems allude to Shakespeare, it is repeatedly the moments in which a Shakespearean character is engaged in imagining that Keats most resourcefully draws upon. Dreamers, actors. Keats does wonders with the cliff that is imagined in *King Lear*, imagined for, even though there is such a thing as Dover Cliff, it is *not there*, not only for one good reason (that this is a play, not a guided tour) but for another: that Edgar is imagining it on his blinded father's behalf, not describing it to his blinded father. The cliff is being imagined, and is doubly imaginary even though there is a real Dover Cliff. "How fearful and dizzy 'tis, to cast one's eyes so low!" The imaginary cliff is dizzying. And so would be the possibility of an extending succession of imaginations within imagination. Fortunately one of the things that a mise-en-scène can effect is the protecting of us against the mise-en-abîme.

It may be said (and was said by me, contemplating *Blind*, *Deaf*, *Adjustment and Work*, and *Multi-handicapped*) that a Wiseman film operates within strict contractual constraints. These people are not actors. These pains are not imaginary. This is what happened. There is such a place. For the performance-films, though, one does need to move an amendment. Some of these people are actors; you will see them acting; you will also see them when not acting; you will also see some people who are not actors. You must imagine away, for the actors and dancers of genius in these films are not only imagined by him, they are imagined into, imagined after, and imagined to. This, even while it is creatively understood that the art of documentary film has further unignorable responsibilities, including the responsibility, well, to *document*.

A coda on coincidence. Praising Wiseman's art those twenty years ago, I wrote of the films' being alive with what an earlier critical idiom called felicities, happenings that will be happily revelatory if we will let them be. Coincidences, if you will. The particular coincidence with which and from which I shall conclude is the matter of my receiving a few weeks ago, from its author, the generous gift of *Manet and the Execution of Maximilian*, by John Elderfield. The historical facts, the artistic facts, Manet's representations and their intriguing evolution, the documentary resources, the evidence of the photographs from Manet's day (I am among the many who had never seen photographs of the firing squad that is the subject of the Manet painting, indeed hadn't realized that they existed) and from our own (all of us have seen the killing of Lee Harvey Oswald, and the gun to the head in Vietnam, and Che Guevara's body), the needed concern with authenticity (can Robert Capa ever be trusted?): all of these come together in a book that is a masterpiece in a medium that, although it is different from Wiseman's, is radiatingly germane to his art. The fact that Elderfield's book came into existence because of an exhibition at MoMA, which has now acquired the entire body of Wiseman's films and is copublishing the present book, is a crowning coincidence. A genius in song has urged, "Take what you have gathered from coincidence." Which is exactly, in his own genius, Wiseman's take.

Author's Note

In writing this essay I have drawn briefly on my essay on Wiseman in Grand Street *(Winter 1989), collected in my book* Reviewery *(Other Press, 2002)—in which I also write on Erving Goffman (originally in* The New York Review of Books, *July 16, 1981) and on Robert Capa (originally in the* Sunday Times, *November 10, 1985). I have a chapter on Keats in* Allusion to the Poets *(Oxford University Press, 2002).*

---

1. An ungainly term, performance-films, and I'd be grateful if someone could think of a term that was equally clear while less clomping.

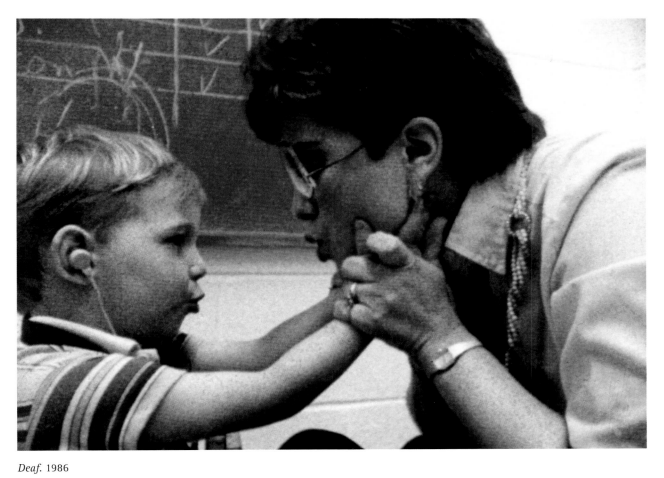

Deaf. 1986

Primate. 1974

The Tawdry Gruesomeness of Reality

Errol Morris

Fred Wiseman has been my idol for a long time. In the 1970s it wasn't all that easy to see his films. For a while I had seen only *Basic Training* (1971) and *High School* (1968). Nothing else. *Titicut Follies* (1967) was almost impossible to see because it was under a court injunction. Videocassettes had been introduced, but Wiseman's films existed only on 16mm—ready to be slapped onto a projector or viewed on a flatbed. Until very recently, he was reluctant to transfer his films to DVD. I believe it was because that would have made them too easy to be seen.

When I was editing my first film, I visited Fred Wiseman in Boston. His offices in those days were on Lewis Wharf, and he very kindly allowed me to watch several of his films on a Steenbeck editing machine. At dinner in his home, one of his sons asked him whether he was going to show me "the two-hour, the three-hour, or the four-hour boring film." Fred didn't smile. But honestly, I had no problem with the length. For me, they could have been even longer.

I saw Fred again at the London Film Festival in 1978. He was showing *Sinai Field Mission*. My future wife, Julia Sheehan, and I went to the first screening at the National Film Theatre. Julia, also a Wiseman fan, had just gotten off an all-night flight from Boston, and promptly fell asleep next to Fred. She was mortified. I remember being mesmerized by the film and its "language." The cinder block buildings, the microwave dishes, and the injunction: to stop sunbathing on the modules. If Surrealist painters had to conjure an empty, featureless plain with pieces of driftwood, Wiseman was able to do away with the driftwood, the conjuring, and simply point the camera at reality. The results are disarming and even dismaying.

One thing surprised me in 1978. Fred had little interest in watching other movies at the festival. He was interested in London theater and excited about the prospect of going to a play. I still believe, over thirty years later, that his movies come from the theater, perhaps the theater of the absurd, rather than from any specific film tradition.

Many people have written or filmed unending paeans to the human race, the nobility of man, the endurance of human spirit. But they have described man as we might

Sinai Field Mission. 1978

the push broom in the middle of the desert, the Texas techies (from some bizarre organization called "E-Systems"), the endlessly marching Ghanaians and Finns, the lonely, enervated one-person basketball games, the bicycle rider straining himself on a hill to nowhere. Sisyphus without the grand illusions. In sum total: a feeling of immense dislocation, meaninglessness, and isolation.

I learned about filmmaking at the Pacific Film Archive in Berkeley, California, where I spent a lot of time watching movies: a few documentaries and a steady diet of Dreyer, Hawks, Renoir, and Nicholas Ray. The documentaries I saw were by Buñuel, Herzog, and Georges Franju—not the Maysles or Leacock and Pennebaker.

Wiseman once asked me, "How could you possibly like my movies? They're all filmed in wobblyscope," his affectionate term for handheld camerawork. And he is right. His movies are stylistically *ur*-vérité. No narration. Available light. Fly-on-the wall. But Wiseman's films prove a simple principle. Style does not determine content. He may be a direct-cinema guy in form, but the content is not valetudinarian but visionary and dystopian. Wiseman has never been a straight vérité "documentarian." He is a filmmaker and one of the greatest we have.

like him to be, with little regard for how he is. Wiseman has had the honesty and supreme decency to portray human society for what it is: a madhouse. *Titicut Follies* was his first but not his only madhouse movie. It was a template for the thirty-eight movies that followed.

I sat down recently and re-watched *Sinai Field Mission*. It was much as I had remembered it. The man with

I have jotted down some obsessions, themes, and predilections that recur in his films. These are not comprehensive but hopefully give some idea of what I love about his work.

1. Surface We constantly think about the motivations of people—their dreams, ideas, hopes. This is not really present in Wiseman's films. He shows things as they are. As they are manifest. He never asks anyone to explain anything, certainly not themselves. He never interviews anybody. Instead he functions as eavesdropper, listening in on conversations unraveling around him . . . And what amazing conversations they are. People endlessly tallying up senseless columns of numbers. There is a brief inkling that the mission in the Sinai is concerned with peacekeeping, that there is perhaps some larger *purpose* for it all, but in this film larger purposes shrink away, leaving us with a residue of meaningless ritual.

2. Real Time We very rarely see examples of real time in the movies. There is the minute of silence in Godard's *Band of Outsiders* (1964). But in Wiseman's films, we are treated to many minutes of silence and to unbroken time. Earnest conversations about seemingly nothing ramble on and on. If movies generally compress time through cutting and editing, then in Wiseman's films time feels extended. A minute of real time can feel interminable, or if you prefer, like an eternity. But I am reminded of a remark made to me by Sidney Coleman, a Harvard quantum field theorist, about the artist and designer Robert Wilson. Sidney said, "Slow is not boring. Only boring is boring." The same could be said about these films. Slow, yes, but endlessly fascinating.

3. Length Fred has gotten into countless fights with film programmers and television producers about the length of his movies. He is the Howard Roark of documentary. Like Ayn Rand's protagonist in *The Fountainhead* (1943), he would rather blow up the building he designed than remove a doorknob. Change one frame, alter one image, try to reduce the length by one second, particularly if it's already over four hours, and Fred will destroy the film rather than compromise. He is the ultimate auteur. *Near Death* (1989) is set in an intensive care unit at Beth Israel hospital in Boston. The viewer begins to feel his own mortality and to wither under the weight of the subject matter over the course of six hours. I, however, told Fred it should have been even longer. I was serious. For a Wiseman film to work it *has* to be long. Unendurably long. Intolerably long. It is hard to look at Wiseman's version of reality. One has to be led there and forced to look at it on a leash with a muzzle.

4. Anti-Sociology Many commentators have written about Fred as though he is a social scientist—a prolific chronicler of institutional behavior. But this gets it backward. Fred likes institutions like Fellini likes the circus. They are a backdrop or a metaphor for something else. I prefer to think of Fred as an entomologist who has poked his camera into some truly nasty termite pile and watches with bemused satisfaction as the termites scurry around carrying odd parcels and such. What are they doing? Can we ever know?

5. Irony Irony is, properly considered, a weapon. Often it's a way of showing a disconnection between what people *think* they are doing and what they *are* doing. Irony abounds in Wiseman's films. No one, absolutely no one, really knows what he is doing. And Wiseman, the observer, is fascinated by a reality (hidden just below the surface) that nobody in the film seems to notice.

6. Religion When Wiseman turns to "evangelical" subjects, as in *Aspen* (1991) and *Essene* (1972) as well as in *Sinai Field Mission*, we characteristically feel the absence of God rather than his presence. The preacher in *Sinai Field Mission* is instructing his soldiers that life has a purpose, that each man fulfills an important and valuable role, but everything he says and the context in which he says it seem to suggest the exact opposite.

7. Sex Dreiser has nothing on him. Sex has never looked as tawdry and sad as it does in a Wiseman film. The lab technicians masturbating a monkey in *Primate* (1974). Humans are portrayed admirably as evil primates. The female veterinarians castrating a wolf in *Zoo* (1993) as a male janitor looks on nervously, his hands folded over his crotch. Fred has a gift for filming condom demonstrations. In *High School II* (1994), white middle-class students are shown how to put a condom on a huge black dildo. In *Public Housing* (1997), the students are black teenage mothers. This time the dildo is small and white.

8. Repetition Every Wiseman scene recalls other Wiseman scenes. Look at *High School* and the hapless teenagers in gym class dancing to "Simon Says" (the 1910

Fruit Gum Company version) and the Ghanaians marching in *Sinai Field Mission*. Wiseman proves that redundancy is the spice of life. Everything recalls everything, but, more to the point, everything repeats everything.

9. The Meaning of Meaninglessness *Sinai Field Mission* . . . a man with a large push broom is sweeping sand in the desert. What more can you say? Oh yes, it's about the UN peacekeeping forces in the Sinai. Trapped inside a windowless bunker and surrounded by a chain-link fence and razor wire, the Texans, Finns, and Ghanaians try to keep the peace. After a short while, they inevitability start fighting with each other. *The Store* (1983) is an excursion into Neiman Marcus during the holiday season. The employee and employer birthday parties at the conclusion are surreal and desperate. Does it matter whether we are rich or poor, owner or lowliest worker? It's all depressing. In *Near Death*, one of the terminal patients explains how she has finally found a way to lose weight. Dying. If you don't pay attention, you might consider the film life affirming. *Essene* takes place in a monastery. A monk pursues a fly unendingly with a flyswatter. This is the height of boredom as religious ecstasy. When a Spanish teacher in *High School* drills in the line, "Sartre is an existentialist philosopher," or

Aspen. 1991

a helpless welfare recipient in *Welfare* (1975) refers to Godot in the closing minutes of the film, I can imagine Wiseman smiling. These are his roots—not Grierson and Flaherty but Beckett, Anouilh, Ionesco, and Sartre, the theater of hopeless irony and the absurd. It's no wonder he lives now in France. Wiseman's films can be considered as extended essays on the meaning of meaninglessness. And they are incredibly bitter and funny. Really, really funny.

These forty-odd films are highly personal and idiosyncratic works. They create a world, equal to the worlds of Renoir and Hitchcock and Fellini. For me, Wiseman is the undisputed king of misanthropic cinema.

Model. 1980

In Memory of Us All:
Some Scenes Out of Wiseman

William T. Vollmann

I once met a brave and experienced white man who with his black wife had done and endured much in the American South for the sake of the civil rights movement. Our encounter took place in Belgrade, where the man had just been intimidated and extorted by his taxi driver. He remarked on his inability to bridge the gap between himself and this tall, angry Serb. Perhaps it would be stretching the case to say that he looked afraid, but he was certainly shaken up and anxious. I marveled over the failure of his competence to transfer into this alien zone. But as a would-be universalist, I myself have so often transformed victory into defeat by ferrying my little accomplishments and knowledges beyond the shelter of their local context. Come to think of it, were they ever worth striving for at all? "We're trying to encourage a ninety-nine-cent jack steak," explains one of the business barons of Frederick Wiseman's *Meat* (1976), and I wonder how far he succeeded in this glori-ous aspiration and whether he has rested on his laurels ever since.

Human lives are little lives, and P. D. Ouspensky's novel *Strange Life of Ivan Osokin* (1915) indicates how dreary it would be to relive our own. As for the lives of other people, their various smallnesses loom far larger than ours, for we comprise (and proudly) that alien infinitude which stifles all triumphs. In *Model* (1980), the very first Wiseman film I saw, I naively expected to find *glamor* (which some American fashion magazines more glamorously spell "glamour"); I in my voyeuristic smallness imagined that I would be entertained or even enchanted by feminine beauty; instead, Wiseman showed me a grind of rejections and retakes. Somebody lacked by an inch the height required for "sophisticated" modeling assignments. Someone's portfolio wasn't adequate. A television commercial of a few seconds' duration required one young woman to project her panty-hosed leg upon various points of an arc, while another model had to descend some steps over and over before the boss-photographer finally conceded she had done it right (and all the while a crowd watched with such reverent pleasure, as if this drudgery for the sake of mercantile fakery could somehow be more special than "real

Meat. 1976

life"). A man and a woman were commanded to collide, over and over, until they met Mr. High and Mighty's standard. The self-satisfied authority of each little tyrant, in other words his certainty, which must have assumed creativity, was frequently rendered ludicrous by his incoherence. He had, let's charitably say, a "vision" of how the model should turn her head, when and where she ought to pause on the steps—or perhaps he didn't; meanwhile he controlled her, and sometimes hectored her, all for the sake of something small. Tell me which outcome would be sadder—for the participants to take pride and pleasure in all this, or for them to participate cynically.

Now for the ninety-eight-cent question: how over-awed is Wiseman with ninety-nine-cent jack steaks? We will never know, for of himself he reveals the minimum, and this merely through our inferences. From his films I take it that he is patient to a fault, that he can wear a forgettable persona (for his subjects seem to forget the camera), that he wishes us to judge what we see almost, but not quite, on our own, that souls of especial interest to him are the self-important, the lost, the high-handed, and the kind, that the life to which he is drawn is that of processes and routines, whether they function rather well, as in *Meat*—whose cattle get rounded up, moved, sold, channeled, driven by the feedlot cowboys shouting "hey" and "hi," then gated, killed, bled, butchered—or somewhat poorly, as in *Welfare* (1975), with its shouting petitioners and arguing staff, not to mention the repetitions of antagonists who cannot listen to each other. Over and over in that latter film we hear people asking: "What am I supposed to do? How can I get through the weekend?" The welfare processors cannot give them any serviceable reply.

And so as I explore Wiseman's oeuvre I come to expect revelations of littleness, and of the wastage of life, by life itself, or by people's incompetence, ineffectiveness, poverty, dullness—or by the regimentations and distortions entailed upon life by *process*. That model descending the steps excites my pity when I see her being made to do it over and over again. Life, so I want to think, should not be like that. It should be "spontaneous." Or should it? *What does Wiseman want me to learn?* His films sometimes meander, and they can even be tedious—necessarily, for they take the trouble to portray the life in and around the entity which they document. Thus in *Welfare* we are treated to a ghastly-hilarious dialogue between the white man, presumably a client, who was recently attacked on the street by black men, and the badge-wearing black man who, like Wiseman himself, continues to be patient with the white man's circularly racist solipsisms. At one moment he informs the black man that he will get a .357 and kill blacks. Even then his interlocutor forbears. But at the end of the day, the black policemen who have endured his provocations for God knows how long put him out the door, then bar it; and from outside he is pounding on it, pathetic, horrible, utterly unable to reason.

That scene still tugs at my memory when I watch *Law and Order* (1969), which may be the most superb of Wiseman's documentaries. Near the beginning, a cigarette-smoking man in a floppy hat declaims on the matter of someone who molested a little girl whom the man in the floppy hat evidently loves. To the policeman he says: "If you guys don't wanna help me I intend to take care of this myself. . . . I would of drug him by his throat, see. . . . If you don't wanna take care of it, I will." And the policeman remains still, patient, listening. I wonder whether in my time and place the policeman would have arrested him for uttering terrorist threats, or at least commanded him to shut up. Later on in *Law and Order* we see a white officer trusting a middle-aged black woman to sit alone in the passenger seat of his police car while he goes out into the rain to find her stolen purse in the weeds; we see her grateful elation and then her realization that even her keys are gone. Rain runs down the windshield as she wonders over and over how she will get into her home.

And as I consider upon these sad scenes, these little scenes, they begin to grow within me, like Chekhov's stories, which upon first acquaintance disguise themselves in random inconsequentiality. That model condemned to go down the steps and down the steps, that old woman who so badly wanted her purse back, got it, and found that the purse alone was not enough—what do their lives say about mine? The shining endurance of the black officer in *Welfare*, who not only puts up with the racist's personalized threats but sometimes engages with them, and even expresses sympathy for and to the man, this is not little at all. It grew out of something drearily overlookable. Something comparable to it is taking place right now, at the welfare office and at the department of motor vehicles and on a bus. And whatever this thing is, perhaps it ought to mean everything to me.

As for that encourager of the ninety-nine-cent jack steak, who was I to belittle him? More or less faithfully he carries out his role, furthering a titanic industrial procedure through which cattle end up in slices at supermarkets; the steps and effects of this procedure are as fascinating as any other ecological web. In it there is grandeur of a sort; there is an overarching end, not necessarily rational but certainly transformative and definitive: those jack steaks will moo no more! What's it all for? Wiseman will not answer. But he will show us the "all." It is up to us to be haunted by it or not.

This all, this everything—what makes it precious? Here is the place to praise a very atypical Wiseman movie (atypical since it is not a documentary at all). *La Dernière Lettre* (*The Last Letter*, 2002) is based on a chapter of one of the greatest twentieth-century novels, Vasily Grossman's *Life and Fate* (1959). Like Wiseman, Grossman was a brave and experienced reporter of facts. He became the very first journalist to publish a report on the Nazi extermination camps.[1] Among the Holocaust's millions of murdered Jews was his mother, whom in *Life and Fate* he transformed from a schoolteacher into a doctor.[2] When I first read this chapter, it moved me deeply, but the novel's immense canvas portrays so many armies, treacheries, terrors, cruelties, and deaths that one more horror could hold me but one ghastly instant. Wiseman, as usual, isolates and slows down that instant, so that what takes only a few minutes to read rivets us for an hour in which the actress Catherine Samie, as the character Anna Semionova, speaks, sings, laughs, and weeps, sometimes accompanied by shadows. ("I originally did it as a play," Wiseman told me, "and I really just used some insignificant modifications. I used the shadows in the play but in a different way than I did in the movie. And the script—the dialogue to the movie is the same as in the play, which is almost exactly the same as in the novel.")[3]

For once, what we see in this Wiseman film is not life as art, but art as life, since Anna Semionova's last letter to her son is a fiction. The scenes are quotidian. Little kindnesses and cruelties, altering mood-landscapes, random verisimilitudes color each descending moment of another industrial procedure through which another ghetto's worth of Jews will end up buried in an antitank trench. Because Anna Semionova realizes what will happen to her, all her perceptions, even the most insignificant, are as treasures—metonyms for the jewel of life itself.

And the quotidian details of Wiseman's documentaries, these are precious in a similar way. They too show us life, pure life, yes, purest life.

Now I spy upon the man in *Hospital* (1969) who is very, very sick; the nurse tries to convince him to stay, because if he leaves he will merely be back, most likely in dangerous condition, but he declines to leave his children, who remain alone in the house. A few years ago, I too checked out of a hospital against medical advice, and the staff spared less than two minutes when they tried to talk me out of it; but the nurse in *Hospital* bears with the man's poor command of English; she takes the trouble to gently but persistently address each of his wish-based arguments: he will just go to a drugstore and get medicine, but, she says, if there were such a medicine, she would have it here and give it to him; he does not want to stay in the hospital, but nobody wants to stay in a hospital; he will not leave his children, but someone else could take care of them—but perhaps there truly is nobody else, and although Wiseman does not let us see how this dialogue ends, it seems probable that the kindly nurse did not prevail.

Here I wonder how much less kindly she might have been in the absence of a camera eye. And the related question: how did Wiseman get the access? Both of these are aspects of the Heisenbergian query: how "real" is what we see? How does the observer's presence affect the observed?

Indeed, the things which Wiseman's subjects do and say are sometimes almost literally incredible. In *Titicut Follies* (1967), the cigarette-smoking doctor who slowly works a force-feeding tube down a patient's nose offers us one of the least disturbing scenes. We are eavesdropping upon a Massachusetts asylum for the criminally insane, where for much of the time and for no reason made explicable to us the men are kept naked. We discover an inmate confessing to a crime; we watch a guard taunting a confused old man into a rage; we overhear a doctor repeatedly interrupting the patient whose sexual practices he is questioning; the doctor badgers him without listening to his answers. How did the camera achieve such inconspicuousness?

Wiseman told me: "I don't know how to answer that question other than that I have big ears and I try to distract some people. It's equally rare that anybody looks at the camera. I suppose that one can't underestimate the vanity of people, but again I don't know what the explanation is."[4]

After all, a degree of complacency is adaptive. Who wouldn't prefer to judge his own actions favorably, even glowingly? This characteristic renders us all easy Wiseman targets. Consider the Beth Israel doctor in *Near Death* (1989) who pretends to leave decisions up to the patient when in actuality he is leading him. Yes, let us please consider and reconsider him, as Wiseman in his quiet way encourages us to do—for what Wiseman provides is *the space around process* which is what we swim in throughout "real life" with its slownesses, repetitions, and randomly unique verisimilitudes. Of course what we see in a Wiseman film has been edited, but gently; pulled up by the roots, but with the dirt left on. When I watch the doctor in *Near Death* give the old man a "choice" regarding whether or not to continue with his many life-sustaining medications in the intensive care unit, it requires precisely this slowness and these repetitions and the old man's particular answers for me to begin to conclude, much against my will, that in fact the doctor is steering him in a certain direction while pretending (perhaps even to himself) not to do so. I call this manipulation. The doctor would probably name it persuasion or education. Once upon a time I had a girlfriend who used to ask me how I thought we were doing, and I would reply that I thought we were doing very well together and that I was happy, at which point she would pause, then inquire if I were really, really sure of that, that she wanted to know how I thought we were *really* doing; then my heart would sink, and I would comprehend that once again she wanted me to be her accomplice in her leaving me. The pleasant young doctor in *Near Death* gives me much the same impression. He asks the old man how he regards his situation. The old man replies. The doctor asks him again. Finally he gets the answer he wants: "Borderline." Now the way will be clear to encourage the old man's consent to withdraw the medication. I think and think and think about this, until I wonder whether in the doctor's place I would do the same thing. Someone is dying, or at least his imminent death is probable. I want to bring this distressing fact to his attention as gently as I can, in order for him to . . . what? In Japan it remains common for an oncologist to assure a terminal cancer patient that he does not have cancer and will hopefully recover. The oncologist may inform the patient's wife, and leave the decision of disclosure up to her. This deceit is kindly meant. So surely is the *Near Death* doctor's little chat with Mr. Borderline. Shouldn't he "face the reality of the situation"? Or is it simply the families who need to face it? In that case the Japanese oncologist is correct. In *Near Death* we watch dedicated people using their medical training to delay death until all the relatives have arrived, or until the family is "ready." One nurse speaks of "the problem of providing too much information to families." She feels resentful (who wouldn't?) when families blame her for a death. They suppose that she needs the patient's bed, or that some selfishness or cruelty of hers ended the beloved life which should have endured forever. She informs us that the family will never be "ready." It took her much study to comprehend in her head and heart and gut just what brain-dead means. An hour-long conference with a distraught family can hardly educate them so thoroughly. I cannot fault this nurse. My own desire to know is nothing more than local prejudice.

After all, another lesson Wiseman teaches us is that most of us don't know much about anything.

In *Law and Order*, the interrogating officer informs his interrogatee of some third-party authority's opinion that "whoever beat this boy is a sadist." "Don't know what that is, either," says the watery-eyed suspect, shaking his head.

Whatever did Wiseman mean in *Law and Order*? Is he for or against police work? Was the film intended to praise the caring patience of some officers, to expose the authoritarian violence of others, or both, or neither? I could have asked this, but in the end I felt, as Wiseman presumably does, that his films should speak to me for themselves, which they most certainly do. For what can they possibly mean but all of the above?

I must admit to being tempted to inquire of the filmmaker how he thought society had changed since he shot the older documentaries. Whenever policemen appear in my parking lot to cite or arrest the homeless Americans who attempt to dwell there, I know not to get too close when I announce myself. There are always two officers, not one as in *Law and Order*, and sometimes they bark at me to stay back; occasionally I can intercede for somebody; mostly the police do whatever they are going to do. I do not blame them; they are overworked. And so they generally do something. Meanwhile, in *Law and Order* inaction is sometimes a police strategy; a fighting couple might be told not to "raise Cain," advised to work matters out between themselves. And my friends who have dealt with today's police concerning stolen vehicles, home burglaries, and the like expressed incredulity (perhaps unfairly) that any cop would take the time to search for a woman's purse in the grass. A woman who used to work for a county mental health program watched *Titicut Follies* with me and was sickened by some of the acts committed by the staff, but she also remarked that in her experience institutions of the kind portrayed "are much more regimented now, due to budget cuts and lower staff-to-patient ratios." I myself perceived a strangely tolerant, even trusting attitude toward the inmates on the part of their keepers, who did not seem worried about the possibility of being assaulted. These clues and others led me toward the conclusion that my own time is more violent, authoritarian, and militarized than before. The Patriot Act and its associated attacks upon the life I like to live make this inference obvious, but it is no less troubling for that.

I do not turn to Wiseman for answers. I trust him to show me neither more nor less than truth regarding whatever scenes he has remembered for us. No one knows where we are going, but noting the samenesses and differences of where we have already been may help us judge how much of the ugliness ahead is necessary, how much consequential. That ugliness itself may be revealed through a kind of beauty is proven by Wiseman's unassuming genius.

1. Front matter for Vasily Grossman, *Life and Fate: A Novel*, trans. Robert Chandler (New York: New York Review of Books, 2006).

2. Chandler, introduction to ibid., p. xxiii.

3. Frederick Wiseman, telephone conversation with the author, February 2010.

4. Ibid.

Law and Order. 1969

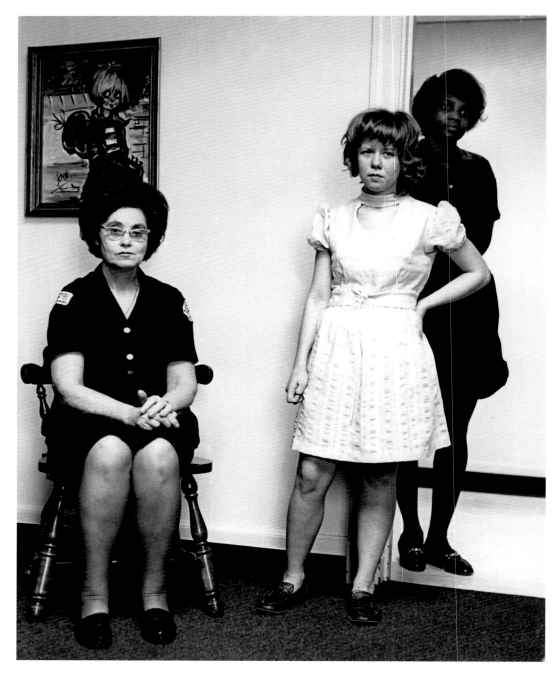

Juvenile Court. 1973

Adjustment and Work. 1986

Hospital. 1969

Central Park. 1989

Missile. 1987

Canal Zone. 1977

Blind. 1986

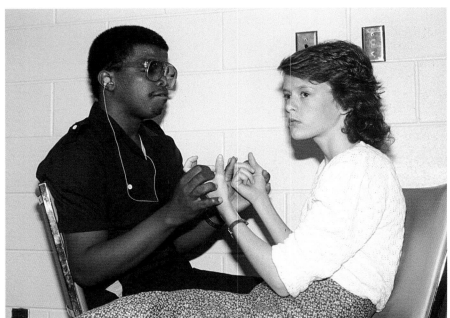

Multi-handicapped. 1986

Zoo. 1993

Titicut Follies. 1967

Learning from Wiseman

Andrew Delbanco

The first film by Frederick Wiseman I saw was *Titicut Follies* (1967). It was the fall of 1969, my freshman year of college, too long ago to trust my memory scene by scene. What I mainly remember is the festive mood in the dining-hall-turned-theater as the lights went down and latecomers ducked under the projector's cone of bluish light as they made their way to sit with friends across the room. A very cool senior had made introductory remarks to the effect that what we were about to see had been "banned in Boston" (always promising), and I think we half-expected the local police to show up as if we had gathered in Rick's gambling den in *Casablanca* (1942). We figured we were in for a couple of "transgressive" hours of the sort we got from movies like *I Am Curious (Yellow)* (1967) or *King of Hearts* (1966)—occasions, mainly, for smoking dope in the dark and feeling sweetly free of "the system." I remember a little snickering during the opening pan across the expressionless faces of the inmates singing "Strike up the Band" while they wave—tentatively, almost spastically—their pompoms. But once the film started, there was only silence in the room, interrupted now and then by a gasp.

A few weeks ago, forty years older, I watched *Titicut Follies* on a DVD on my computer screen in my study at home. Memories of that first viewing came flooding back: the guards tormenting an inmate named Jim, marching him naked up and down the bright-lit hallways, peppering him with variations on one relentless question: "How's that room, Jim? . . . You gonna keep that room clean, Jim? . . . How's that room gonna be tomorrow, Jim? . . . How come it's not clean today?" until he screams out his compliance in rage and helplessness. There was the agitated inmate, head bobbing, pouring out, like Lucky in *Waiting for Godot*, strings of nonsense and newscaster phrases ("Ben-Gurion government . . . I am called Christ Jesus . . . I am called a Borgia . . . black Muslims . . . no good, we send back to England to my sister there . . . President Johnson"), interrupting each intelligible fragment with a burst of gibberish—"biddledepuh, biddledegah"—until he wraps it all up with, "Come in, Mr. President Johnson, and order my release." And then there was the German psychiatrist who looks for all the world like Hermann Göring, pestering an inmate with questions in a monotone voice about how often he masturbates. Did he feel guilty after raping his own child? "I need help but I don't know where I can get it," says the young man, handsome and fit, but with a deadness in his eyes. "You get it here, I guess," says the doctor—help, as the rest of the film makes clear, in the form of lockdowns, hosings, strip searches, and assorted other humiliations.

Back in my college days everyone was reading R. D. Laing, father of the "anti-psychiatry" movement (*The Politics of Experience* [1967]), Thomas Szasz (*The Myth of Mental Illness* [1960]), and, soon to supersede them as an academic staple, Michel Foucault (*Madness and Civilization* [1961]), all of whom, in one way or another, attacked prevailing ideas of what was "normal" and what was "sick." We were casually throwing around Erving Goffman's phrase "total institution" to include schools and hospitals—as if the whole society were a gulag in which the real crazies were not the deviants or delinquents but the people in charge who deemed them so. We spoke about "soft coercion" and consciousness-raising, and regarded Wiseman's films—not only *Titicut Follies* but also *High School* (1968), *Hospital* (1969), and *Basic Training* (1971)—as advancing "the movement," whatever, exactly, that was.

Yet however much Wiseman may have made the film in a spirit of outrage at how the patients—really inmates—were treated at Bridgewater State Hospital, he had invited us to a freak show. We were affluent late adolescents for whom it was impossible to think that the men on-screen had anything to do with us. We watched with a mixture of prurience and pity. The frequent frontal nudity—one of the pretexts for banning the film—gave us a frisson of sophistication as we pretended not to be shocked. Starting with the follies themselves, we were poised between laughter and horror as the guard, presiding as master of ceremonies, presents the chorus line as if he were doing an Ed Sullivan impression. Then, as the film moved into the cellblock itself, it felt as if we were looking through a peephole at things we were not meant to see, or as my college contemporary Wendy Lesser nicely put it, at "things we don't want to acknowledge we want to know."[1]

Watching the film today is an utterly different experience. I see images of Abu Ghraib. I see failed men exposed to mockery for having failed, men who once had families and jobs and respectable credentials, but, unable to manage their sexual or violent urges, descended into the pit into which any of us might fall. When I first saw the scene of Jim being shaved, I had not yet witnessed my father—who delighted me as a child by letting me watch him lather his face in the morning—lying prone in his final hospital bed, being shaved by a nurse not much more concerned with doing it thoroughly or gently than the barbering guard in the film was.

"The real film," Wiseman has said, "takes place where the mind of the viewer meets the screen," and if I try to revisit that middle ground as it existed when I first went there, I can't.[2] Upon a recent re-viewing of Wiseman's next work, *High School*, about a large public school in Philadelphia, I felt the same disjunction between then and now. When it was first released, it gave my generation a view through the peephole at ourselves, or at least recent versions of ourselves. I remember feeling superior to the boys with soft mustache hair and not quite fully deepened voices. I remember the scene in which a teacher patrols the halls demanding a hall pass from every student he encounters—a squat little Nazi of whom Wiseman gives us the posterior view (not flattering) as the camera follows him from behind. The teachers, I recall, seemed to have been cut more or less from the same cloth as the Bridgewater guards—impatient and remote, going through the motions until closing hour.

It was all very different from the private high school from which I had just been graduated, and yet it felt familiar. Some of my own teachers had been at the school for decades and were, as the phrase goes, out of touch; others—young women just out of college or young men evading the draft—seemed just a step ahead of us in life. So when I watched the two English teachers in *High School*—first, the matronly woman with bad teeth reading aloud "Casey at the Bat," then the young woman with a Joan Baez haircut talking with almost erotic intensity about Paul Simon's "Dangling Conversation"—it was, for ill or good, like being back in school again.

But now that I've watched it as a teacher myself, it's a different film. I feel for the teachers, all of them. I sense the pressure of the "counterculture" pushing from outside the school as they deliver sex-ed and deportment lessons while the students, seething at these surrogate parents yet frightened of their own impending freedom, sense that they are on the verge of a new world in which the old norms won't apply. The teachers—though doubtless less reflective than those in Wiseman's later film *High School II* (1994), about a charter school in Harlem—seem to be trying their best, as when one of them, Dr. Allen, explains to a student indignant over having been punished with a detention that to be a man means to prove "you can take orders."

High School. 1968

MICHAEL: I should prove that I'm a man and that's what I intend to do by doing what I feel, in my opinion, is what I am doing is right.

DR. ALLEN: Are you going to take your detention or aren't you? I feel that you should.

MICHAEL: I'll take it, but under protest.

DR. ALLEN: All right, then. You take it under protest. That's good.

And then there is the poignant pair of scenes with the distraught father who comes to school to protest his daughter's poor grades. Bursting out of a suit that might once have fit him, he seems to be wearing an emblem of his superannuation. A few scenes later, we see him at a college-counseling session with his daughter and wife, pushing back against the girl's wish to go to cosmetology school instead of to a proper college. His anger sprays out in multiple directions: at the school for underestimating his daughter, at her for expecting so little of herself, and even, I think, at himself, for his failure to steer her toward the life he hopes for her—a hope, destructive as it may be, that arises out of love.

So I have changed. But so, I think, has Wiseman. Since the late 1960s, he has been making movies at a pace of roughly one per year—all the more astonishing since he typically shoots over a hundred hours to yield anywhere from ninety minutes in the final cut (*Basic Training*) to six hours (*Near Death* [1989]), sometimes spending more than a year in the editing room. "The shooting is the research," he has said.[3] He begins with no a priori story or point of view, but he disavows the term "cinéma vérité," which he considers both specious and pretentious. He prefers "reality fiction"—a term that registers how much is shaped by the choices of what to shoot and how to put together what remains after the radical cutting. He uses no narrator, yet his aim is not to be objective but to be, to use the word he prefers, fair. In all these respects he has managed for more than forty years to be consistent without being redundant.

Yet he has become a more profound artist, and I don't just mean that he has become more adept at his craft. As the film historian Barry Keith Grant points out, the use of sound in *Titicut Follies* (Wiseman's first film) was already very controlled: we get thick ambient noise in the harrowing scene of an inmate being force-fed, then total silence when the same man is shown a few moments later as a corpse.[4] It's not so much that Wiseman has surpassed his early technique as that his pace and tone have changed. He lingers, savors; he has become more interested in aesthetic expression, both as a subject (notably in the two films about dance, *Ballet* [1995] and *La Danse—Le Ballet de l'Opéra de Paris* [2009]) and as an aspiration for what he hopes to achieve through his own art. He has become a filmmaker less interested in exposé than in revelation.

The turn is evident, to my eye at least, in his beautiful film of 1999, *Belfast, Maine,* in which there is a palpable simultaneity of intimacy and loneliness—as expressed by a recurring shot of cars driving urgently at dusk past shuttered shops or darkened houses. We visit the nerve centers of the town: the courtroom, school, town hall, church, where we witness legal pleadings, an English class, a debate over tax assessments, prayers for the dying and the dead. In the interstices of these scenes we get fleeting images that have a shimmer of allegory: skewered fish wriggling in their death throes, a man pushing leaves off his lawn—as likely to win his battle against the wind as Sisyphus is to roll his stone over the hill.

There are witty touches: a policeman stops by the "Wistful Vista" antique store to check that it's locked up tight; General Patton looks out from a *Life* magazine photo over the shoulder of a high school English teacher who extols the virtues of Captain Ahab. In fact, the film opens with a montage that seems somewhere between kitsch and irony—the harbor at dawn, gulls in the mist, the sounds of lapping water and the engines of lobster boats—and that we expect to lead into some human story ashore to which birds and sun and sea are utterly indifferent.

But that's not quite what we get. Instead, we get fragments of stories, unlinked except by proximity in the town of Belfast and in the universe of the film itself. Yet one of the amazing effects of this film, despite the absence of conventional narrative and the extended length (more than four hours), is its considerable suspense. As we watch workers engaged in handicraft or automated labor, Wiseman has some fun with us: what on earth are they making? Long before dawn, a man arrives at a dark coffee shop, unlocks and sets up, rolling and baking dough, turning and pounding . . . It's only when he gets to cutting the holes that we realize he is making donuts. We visit fish- and potato-processing plants. Decapitated sardines travel down a conveyor belt to their ultimate destination in roll-top cans; potatoes are washed and steamed, the flesh scooped out and frozen en route to the supermarket as packaged patties topped with paprika. The machinery sputters and groans

High School II. 1994

like antique tractors at a country fair. I suspect that future viewers will turn to this film as a documentary record of the United States in its late-industrial phase.

But Wiseman is not primarily a social commentator or an investigator of this or that institution, as he is often said to be. He is a portraitist, and his favorite genre is the double portrait. A visiting nurse washes the feet of a diabetic old man. A woman picks lice from another woman's hair. In most such scenes—I am tempted to call them duets or *pas de deux*—one person occupies the subsidiary position (student, patient, novice, recruit) while the other (teacher, doctor, drill sergeant, nurse) holds the authority. In the early films, there can be cruelty in this relation, but in the later work Wiseman seems more interested in unarticulated tenderness, or what is sometimes called tough love.

Belfast, Maine includes two extraordinary instances of teaching inspired by love—love of the subject as well as of the learner. A young choirmaster speaks to his choristers about Bach and Palestrina, and suddenly we see in their faces that they understand the music in a new way. The high school teacher speaking to his students about *Moby-Dick* credits Melville with rendering ordinary fishermen—he knows he is speaking to the children

of fishermen—as heroes capable of courage and grandeur. These are moving demonstrations of what genuine teaching can be, in a film where we meet many teachers: the nurses and social workers who treat the dying, but also the dying who teach the living what's in store for them and how best to bear it.

Frederick Wiseman seems to me a great teacher himself. He not only shines light into places we are not meant to go, but he shows us anew places whose familiarity has made them obscure to us. In this sense he puts me in mind of Emerson's remark that "the whole secret of the teacher's force" is the power to "get the soul out of bed, out of her deep habitual sleep, out into God's universe."[5] This image of the teacher as exasperated parent shaking awake the somnolent child and shooing him out the door captures for me what Wiseman is all about. In his early films, one feels a certain anger: wake up, wake up, he seems to say, to who we really are and what we do to one another. In the later films, the shaking is gentler; he invites us to come out into the world to see the beauty and compassion we would otherwise miss. Emerson is apposite again: "The invariable mark of wisdom is to see the miraculous in the common."[6] We are all in Wiseman's debt for clearing our sight.

1. Wendy Lesser, "Unwise Restrictions," *The Threepenny Review*, no. 48 (Winter 1992): 25.

2. Frederick Wiseman, interview by Charlie Rose, PBS, January 27, 2010.

3. Ibid.

4. Barry Keith Grant, introduction to Grant, ed., *Five Films by Frederick Wiseman* (Berkeley and Los Angeles: University of California Press, 2006), p. 6.

5. Ralph Waldo Emerson, journal entry, April 20, 1834, in *Emerson in His Journals*, ed. Joel Porte (Cambridge, MA: Harvard University Press, 1982), p. 123.

6. Ralph Waldo Emerson, "Nature," 1836, in *Selections from Ralph Waldo Emerson*, ed. Stephen E. Whicher (Boston: Houghton Mifflin, 1957), p. 55.

Belfast, Maine. 1999

Titicut Follies. 1967

Comfort for the Tough-Minded

David Denby

When I met Fred Wiseman, in the fall of 1969, in Cambridge, Massachusetts, he was working in his own urban planning company. "Working" may not be the right phrase; "temporarily hiding" might be closer to the truth. I'm absolutely sure that by then, with *Titicut Follies* (1967), *High School* (1968), and *Law and Order* (1969) behind him, he had committed himself to a life as a documentary filmmaker and artist. Certainly his earlier life of teaching and service was drawing to a close: his impatience with anything else but filmmaking was obvious enough. I have just used the word "artist," but I will quickly add that he did not on that occasion—or any other—refer to himself that way. In fact, he is generally loath to say detailed things about his work at all. In this reticence, which is produced, of course, not by humility but by pride, he is similar to another American director who is almost exactly the same age, Clint Eastwood. In both cases, the work does almost all the speaking that matters; description and evaluation are left to others.

As I remember, when I showed up at his office, I was expecting to find someone angry and highly political. Both the scandalous inadequacy of the facility for the criminally insane in *Titicut Follies* and the punitive banality of the Philadelphia public high school in *High School* led me to imagine an ardent crusader for reform, an antagonist to the institutional forms of life in capitalist America. Those impressions weren't entirely wrong; they were just inadequate. Wiseman's career as a filmmaker is a stunning case of what might be called the artistic uses of anger. There is, without doubt, an extraordinary rage hidden deep in the underbrush of many of the films, but it does not emerge as an ideologue's rant. Wiseman never uses narration, explanatory titles, music, or commentary of any sort. He is stubbornly unhelpful; he will not shape, in any easy way, our responses to his films. Instead, out of the many hours of film (and now digital video) that Wiseman shoots in any given institution, he creates an elaborately patterned mosaic of scenes that suggest not only the life of the hospital, police force, housing complex, school, or boxing gym that is his subject, but also his own complicated response to it. As he would be the first to admit (on this subject he is eloquent), his response is always subjective. It cannot be anything else. A filmmaker is not omniscient, and he exercises taste and judgment every time he focuses on one matter rather than another. The final edited version of the footage is a representation of what he has experienced, observed, and felt. The choice and arrangement is always subjective.

But, my God, how rich a subjectivity! Wiseman's films can bring one close to tears or rage, anguish or exhilaration, exasperation or intense happiness. He has a mischievous, sometimes black sense of humor that plays through all the films. And anger is certainly one of the emotions in play. But the anger, when it emerges, is directed not only at a failing institution or at injustice, but often at the sheer difficulties of life, the sometimes intractable nature of our common social existence, the sometimes intolerable nature of our common physical existence. There is no more exquisitely sensitive movie than *Near Death* (1989), his six-hour film about terminally ill patients in a Boston hospital. The patients move inexorably to the end, but Wiseman doesn't rush anything. They are given the dignity of the final struggles, the final decisions; the doctors explain the options, to the patients and their families. The movie sets up a paradox: taking the patients off life-sustaining machines is the only way toward health, and yet, without the help of those machines, the patients will probably die. Through-

out his career, Wiseman has looked plainly and evenly at such double binds; he has looked plainly and evenly at many things that are difficult in life. He does so without offering some higher meaning or philosophical consolation; he does not, in the manner of most religions, attempt to soften what is unacceptable. He offers spirituality without illusion. What do I mean by spirituality? If suffering can be "redeemed," he has done so by openly acknowledging it, observing it, and trying to understand it. There is comfort in his films in the form of understanding, but you have to be strong to feel it. Let us call it comfort for the high-spirited and tough-minded. For a high-spirited man or woman, anger is part of his or her relation to the nature of life.

That he was a complicated man, not too easily understood, I saw in our first meeting. There was, first of all, his appearance, with its alternating resemblance to a 1950s folksinger or radical nightclub comic, or perhaps a Jewish leprechaun of some fantastic variety. He had a high, large forehead topped (then) by a full head of lengthy and tousled dark hair, seemingly enormous eyes, a narrowing chin, an overall air of faint mockery. He was quizzical, alert, friendly but not, it was obvious, openly eager for anyone's approval. I quickly realized that anything approaching rhetoric or even generalization would be

Domestic Violence. 2001

greeted with a pause, a smile, and a stare, as if he were waiting for you to hear the emptiness of your own words. If some statement or sentiment voiced by someone else came up in conversation, and he disliked it, there would be an abrupt laugh and perhaps the passing judgment of "bullshit." Every writer and director, of course, believes that he is in possession of what Hemingway said was necessary to an artist—a "built-in bullshit detector." To believe that one has it, however, is not the same thing as actually having it; nor is it the same as being free of bullshit oneself. (I'm not sure, for instance, that Hemingway was aware of his own dishonesties, particularly as he got older.) Wiseman, however, as far as I can see, is free of the usual vanities and delusions. His clarity is temperamental and pragmatic; he's sure that he can't afford to be stupid. Yet this toughness is not accompanied by the usual cynicism and derision expressed by people who pride themselves on never being taken in. Hope lies in the underbrush of his movies too.

In the last forty-one years, I have met him many times, and I have talked to him on the telephone quite a bit, but the impressions I formed then of his temperament haven't changed at all. What immediately became apparent was his rare combination of patience and stubbornness. He has never altered his working methods—never enlarged the size of his crew, or cut down the amount of footage he takes, or discovered any shortcuts to getting his meaning across. Some audiences have been dismayed by the extreme length of films like *Near Death*, *Welfare* (1975), or *High School II* (1994), but Wiseman's feeling is that there is no way to dramatize the complicated situations that people find themselves in without running conversations and conflicts at length. For Wiseman, time has an almost moral component. It turns out that one of the worst things that the insulted and the injured face is that no one will give them much time. They have woes, they have stories; they want recognition, yet very few hard-pressed bureaucrats, welfare workers, or drug counselors will listen at length to their complaint, their history. But Wiseman has the time. If you pay close attention, the drama of these prolonged episodes increases, rather than decreases, as the scene goes on—for instance, the interview with an addicted resident of the Ida B. Wells project in *Public Housing* (1997) or the long opening scene between a quarrelsome couple at the beginning of *Domestic Violence* (2001). In such scenes, an entire way of life opens up. We see the tangle and complication of another person's existence, the intractability of relationships—something we thought we would rather not know about. For the audience, attitude gives way to understanding, irritation to gratitude.

Wiseman's patience extends to the people on the other side of the institutional divide—the cops, nurses, doctors, social and welfare workers, political organizers, and all the other men and women who do difficult, often thankless work day after day. Wiseman, it turns out, is poet of the unheralded people of good will; he joins the temperament of an artist to the idealism of the best people who keep American society running. Throughout the films, there are fleeting impulses of caring, sympathy, solidarity, a welling-up of kindness even in the bleakest circumstances. In 1969, when Wiseman made *Law and Order*, conventional liberal opinion was very hostile to urban police forces—"the pigs" who protected property and the powerful and oppressed the poor. This attitude, of course, is not entirely false. But it's drastically incomplete. In *Law and Order*, which was shot in the Midwestern city of Kansas City, there were certainly a few brutal cops who pushed people around. But most of the time, the police found themselves intervening in incoherent and violent family arguments. What should they do? They arrived at the end of a long string of social and personal failure—inadequate parents, bad schools, too few jobs, too much drink and drugs. The police were the last resort, and nothing in their training prepared them for this role; they often arrived just as violence was about to break out. Years later, in *Public Housing*, a slightly officious cop threatens a young woman just standing on the street in Chicago. What is she up to? He tells her to pull herself together. He's patronizing, but his experience suggests to him that if she's standing in the same spot for hours, she's either selling drugs or hooking. It's possible, of course, that she simply has nowhere to go. The moment is ambiguous, but, in his own way, the cop is trying to keep her out of trouble. In the same film, two other cops are very gentle with a confused old man who is being evicted from the projects. Later, a drug addict being hounded by enemies (presumably people he owes money to) sits down outside a police station, his back against the wall. He won't move, this bewildered anchorite, and a gentle cop, who knows he's been taking drugs, lets him sit there. The addict seeks a moment of refuge, a place to avoid annihilation.

What has distinguished Wiseman from facile humanism or mere sympathy is a streak of what can only be called black comedy. Everyone who knows his movies has a favorite moment. I remember all too well that episode in *Titicut Follies* when a doctor is force-feeding an inmate who refuses to eat. The doctor pours something liquid into a funnel attached to a narrow hose, which is inserted into the throat of a howling and shaking old man. After forty-three years, I can still see that ghastly image, in which the doctor's cigarette is fixed in his mouth (both hands are busy), its lengthening ash dangling precipitously over the open funnel. The hanging ash suggests insolence and indifference, of course, but it's also grotesquely funny. So is a scene in *Public Housing* in which a jolly nurse gives a lecture on condoms to unmarried young women who, in some cases, already have babies howling in the background of the room. A second child would be financially disastrous, so the birth-control lesson might yet be valuable, but the scene is still funny. Wiseman has an infallible eye for contradictions, absurdities; he will catch anyone whose rhetoric doesn't fit the situation he has to deal with. *Welfare*, which I've often thought is Wiseman's greatest film, gives full account of the messes that poor people can get caught up in; they are sent around from one office to another, and they press forward with powerful choral laments. In such cases, the anger is directed less at social arrangements than at the nature of life, which, at its most harrowing, can be inexorably comical. In spirit, Wiseman at such moments is close to such artists as Kafka and Tadeusz Borowski.

At times the black comedy fuels a powerful irony—in, say, *Canal Zone* (1977), where the Americans at a soon-to-be-terminated colony console themselves for their distance from the United States with endless patriotic displays, as if they had to be more American than mainlanders. In *The Store* (1983), the sales clerks use snobbish appeals to sell luxury goods to wealthy but culturally insecure Texans. I don't believe that Wiseman, in any of these movies, is engaged in simple rug-pulling. There is always a strong tinge of sympathy, or at least acceptance of weakness or need. In *Aspen* (1991), he does not, as you would expect, satirize the liberal intellectuals who gather there for high-minded conferences, or the wealthy tourists who show up to ski. Most of the movie, as far as I can tell, is about the year-round residents. Such people live amid transcendent beauty (the frequent, stunning shots of the mountains make that clear), yet we find them seeking transcendence not in nature but in religious services, in counseling and group therapy, in quack medical cures, in cosmetic treatments and surgery. They grasp for comfort. Their repeated assertion that God is everywhere, we begin to think, is produced by the hidden fear that God is nowhere. There is an element of satire in all this, but also a ready sympathy. People, we can see, need community and reassurance even amid the greatest splendor.

If Wiseman has never flinched before the terrors of poverty, illness, emptiness, unhappiness, he has also celebrated communities that work—the tenant-rights organizers and the men who take care of other people's children in *Public Housing*, the teachers prodding and challenging their students in *High School II*. Set in a good public school in Southeast Harlem, where the student body is forty-five percent black, forty-five percent Latino, and only ten percent white, the movie is a study in multiethnic liberalism as a success—and as the only sane educational method in a society like the United States. Again and again the teachers demand evidence, reason, appreciation of different perspectives. They are incisive without sarcasm—a kind of pedagogic ideal. At the same time, they try to deal with the violence of the surrounding community as it affects the school and the behavior of the kids. In the original *High School*, from 1968, the school was anxiously trying to keep order amid social change and to bottle up the kids' sexuality; they pounded the students into shape. The extraordinary increase in understanding and effectiveness expressed by the teachers and administrators in the second film makes one think that progress really is possible.

As I got to know Wiseman better, I was not surprised to learn that he was a hedonist who loved food, theater (more than movies), skiing, conversation, old jokes, gossip, and all the other pleasures of social life. His wife—law professor Zipporah Wiseman—tells me that he will never sell his house in Cambridge. It is filled with the thousands of books (literature and poetry most especially) that he loves. The affable, sociable side of Wiseman has moved into his recent work. He has celebrated the language of fiction (*La Dernière Lettre* [*The Last Letter*, 2002]), great American and French ballet companies (*Ballet* [1995]; *La Danse—Le Ballet de l'Opéra de Paris* [2009]), and the great French repository of theatrical tradition (*La Comédie-Française* [1996]). In all this activity, there is nothing of the noble martyr struggling against a semi-indifferent public—the common pose of many serious documentary makers—but only a happy commitment to work, an unceasing productivity which has now yielded thirty-six films in forty-three years. (Actually, thirty-nine films if you include the three unreleased at this writing, *The Garden* [filmed 2004], *Boxing Gym* [2010], *and Le Crazy Horse* [2011].) This body of work, in its variety and richness, its humor and open acceptance of tragedy as well as pleasure, is an achievement unrivalled in documentary in our time.

Welfare. 1975

Frederick Wiseman and Catherine Samie during the filming of
La Dernière Lettre (*The Last Letter*). Paris. 2001

Interview with Catherine Samie

January 11, 2010

MARIE-CHRISTINE DE NAVACELLE: You told me the other day that Fred Wiseman is a predator of humanity. Could you tell me what you meant by that?

CATHERINE SAMIE: It's true. He looks at what's happening in the world . . . we're all so warped. He has a lot to choose from! He captures the comic, painful, terrifying situations of life.

MCN: But why do you use the term "predator"?

CS: Because he takes!

MCN: He steals?

CS: No, he doesn't steal, he takes. It's in front of him, so he takes it. He has curiosity, an eye.

MCN: There is something destructive in the term "predator."

CS: I don't think so. He seizes a situation, he takes it, films it, assembles it, constructs it. Sometimes I say to him: "Mr. Wiseman, it's magnificent, but it's too long." He says, "No." I say, "It's too long." "No." "It's too long." "No."

MCN: You're going to make his friends laugh.

CS: It's true, there's nothing you can do, because he's a passionate observer. He has these enormous ears, you can really grab on to them. When I say, "Hello, Mr. Wiseman," I grab his ears.

MCN: Oh, really?

CS: Yes, it reassures me. And he has these eyes that are upturned, like the paintings of saints in churches, you know, with the whites of the eyes showing underneath—he's always in a state of ecstasy. He has a virginal side, and a totally diabolical side. The ears are rather surprising, but the expression in his eyes is . . . approaching the Divine?

MCN: It's true. I noticed the ears, but the eyes . . .

CS: He's a man who observes humanity. He is sometimes rather cruel . . . he goes *ha ha ha ha*. He laughs like the devil.

MCN: Is that irony?

CS: No, no, no, no. He doesn't laugh from his solar plexus, out of a need to laugh. No, no, no, he goes *ha ha ha* . . . a small thing like that. I can't describe it. It's high-pitched.

MCN: You're introducing me to aspects of Fred I hadn't seen.

CS: He's someone who came into my life, and offered me two texts, *La Dernière Lettre* and *Oh les beaux jours*.[1]

MCN: You didn't know him before?

CS: I met him when he made the documentary on the Comédie-Française, of which I was doyenne at the time. He filmed me a lot, in various situations, committees, rehearsals, life in the house of Molière, official visits, the retirement home.[2]

MCN: You don't think that's a film?

CS: No, Mr. Wiseman, your *reportage* . . .

MCN: You just said you find his films too long. What did you think of *Near Death* [1989], which goes on for six hours?

CS: Not for death, no, no, not for death—the subject matter doesn't allow one to say, "It's too short, it's too long," that's not true. It's such an important moment for all of us on this earth. We all ask that big question: what do you do at that moment, whatever happens, what happens? Is Mr. Wiseman filming you at that moment, passing to the other side? You never know!

MCN: That would be a lucky chance.

CS: Yes, it'll happen, it'll happen . . .

MCN: The filmmaker Henri Storck said that there were two things one could not show in a documentary film, people dying or making love.[3] Perhaps he was right, it's hard. But in *Near Death*, Wiseman does not film death directly.

CS: He films the moments that happen, the entourage, the people who accept it, who don't accept it, who wait.

MCN: The family, the medical staff.

CS: The sorrow.

MCN: So you don't think that film is too long?

CS: No, not that one, no. The film I loved—really loved—was *Titicut Follies* [1967]. To me, it's Mr. Wiseman's greatest film. Everything was there, in front of him: humanity, these men's cries for help, the set, the text . . . He's the one making discoveries, he's the one turning them into images and giving them to other people. Deeply shattering. He's . . . he's an observer, a taker, a worker.

MCN: And also a giver.

CS: Yes. He gives to others. I take and I give. You'll see what you'll see, I'll illuminate it, and you'll see. In any case, I think so. That's his way of filming the world and understanding it.

MCN: So while filming you during the shooting of *La Comédie-Française* [1996] he wanted to work with you?

CS: Yes. Jean-Pierre Miquel, who was the administrator of the Comédie-Française, and Mr. Wiseman came to see me with the text of *La Dernière Lettre*. They said, "Do you want to read this text? Do you want to do it?" I said yes. I couldn't do otherwise. I experienced the war; I've seen horror. I was eight years old. I saw people against a wall, shot just like that; I saw my schoolmate thrown to the ground, pulled by the hair; the SS. Screaming, pain, fear. Fears and tears. The horror. My last name is Samie; I'm not Jewish, but I saw the war, I saw all those children, all those women . . . I can't forget that, I can't forget that suffering, because although I didn't experience great suffering, they experienced it.

MCN: You said regarding *La Dernière Lettre* that you were not acting but witnessing. That's what you just described in a way.

CS: I didn't act. The text is extremely impressive. It requires great concentration, a lot of calm, and suffering. Mr. Wiseman lit it very, very well, with shadows. It was the most beautiful set that ever was. I was alone, but there were all the deportees, walking . . .

MCN: Did Wiseman give a lot of direction?

CS: He likes that; it's his uptight, predatory side. He's somewhat stubborn.

MCN: But, for instance, does he give you indications about how to say the text, or make the gestures?

CS: Yes, yes, he said: That—yes; that—no, not like that. He helped me in *La Dernière Lettre*. He gave me photos of James Stewart, Cary Grant, Gary Cooper—you know, those sublime men.

MCN: So he brought you photos.

CS: Yes. We rehearsed in a room where there was a large fireplace. I was in front of the fireplace. Then as I spoke to my son, he put up several photos, so that my eyes changed direction, several photos of these magnificent stars, and I spoke to my son, who took the form of James Stewart or Cary Grant or Gary Cooper. That's your son, look, it's Vitia. That's Vitia. So then I looked at Vitia, I spoke to Vitia. Go to the other Vitia, there. I still have those photos. I kept them.

MCN: Wiseman has said that in the theater, unless you're in the first three rows, you can't see the actors' faces, but that in the cinema, the filmmaker chooses what he wants to show the viewer, which is to say, in the film, for example, he chose to show your face and hands.

CS: Yes, one always relies on the director. In the cinema even more than in the theater. In a film, he can make you appear or disappear, it's extraordinary; what's more, it's crazy. You can be magnificent and not be present on-screen at that moment, because the director sees his film another way or imagines it another way. Giorgos Arvanitis was a magnificent cinematographer for *La Dernière Lettre*.[4]

MCN: Yes, those images are very beautiful. We talked a lot about *La Dernière Lettre*, but I still have a question. You say—and it must often be true in the cinema—that it was difficult to preserve the intensity of your character for the film, because there were interruptions.

CS: We spent several days filming.

MCN: And for you, in relation to your acting . . .

CS: Ah, it was hard, because we had to start all over. For the play, when we were performing at the Studio-Théâtre, around six thirty, seven o'clock, there was a sort of regularity, like in the convent. I had my concentration time in my loge, my habits, my vocal exercises. I could try to start again, because you have to get the instrument started. For me, it didn't happen that way.

And it was terrible, at times, learning the text; I couldn't do it. I cried and cried. I had to stop crying, of course; nevertheless, it was very painful, because not only was there the problem of the war, genocide, our humanity, the problem of the Jews of this time, but also the problem of [*trails off*].

The text is great, because it's a mother, so in the theater, there are girls, there are boys, there are young people, there are old people, but they all have a mother they either got along with or didn't. There are tender mothers with big bosoms; we have memories of nuzzling into that warmth, just like that, that tenderness, to reassure ourselves. It's true. There are some who spend all their life chasing that, some who never had it; it concerns everyone. The only thing I didn't understand is when I presented the film in Casablanca, it was terrible.

MCN: In what sense?

CS: Because there were immediately two or three women in the theater who screamed, "Why are you playing this? It's a drama about a Jewish mother, and you never think about the Palestinians." I said, "Ma'am, that's not true, it's the same thing; this is a mother, a mother has no borders, no country . . ."

MCN: We've talked about *La Dernière Lettre*, but there is also *Oh les beaux jours*.

CS: Well, it's a love story that Mr. Wiseman absolutely wanted to start with me again; I was stupefied to see this man so attached to my body [*laughs*]. I'm talking about my body, because it's my instrument.

MCN: There you're already buried at the start.

CS: Yes, it was a relief for him [*laughs*].

MCN: And what sort of impression did this mise-en-scène leave you with?

CS: It was very difficult, very, very difficult. Me, I was at the end of my expression, theater, when I finished acting in *Oh les beaux jours*. For the last time in my life, I performed—in Martinique, I think—at nine o'clock in the morning. It was a final memory, like that, of the theater, with Mr. Beckett.

MCN: I would like to end with Fred Wiseman. Would you be prepared to work with him again?

CS: Ah, yes, if he asked me to.

Translated from French by Jeanine Herman

1. In 2000, in the Studio-Théâtre, Paris, Catherine Samie performed *La Dernière Lettre* (*The Last Letter*), an adaptation of a chapter from Vasily Grossman's novel *Life and Fate* (1959), directed by Frederick Wiseman for the Comédie-Française. In 2002, she and Wiseman made a film based on this text, and with the same title. The film was an official selection of the 2002 Cannes Film Festival. In 2006–07, at the Théâtre du Vieux-Colombier, Paris, Samie performed in Samuel

Beckett's *Oh les beaux jours* (*Happy Days*), also directed by Wiseman for the Comédie-Française.

2. The retirement home where Samie, as doyenne of the Comédie-Française, visited former actors in the company.

3. Henri Storck (1907–1999) was the Belgian filmmaker who, with Joris Ivens, made *Misère au Borinage* (1933).

4. The cinematographer Giorgos Arvanitis is originally from Greece, where he became known for his work with the director Theo Angelopoulos. Since moving to France in 1989, he has worked with many international filmmakers, including Catherine Breillat.

La Dernière Lettre (*The Last Letter*). 2002

Essene. 1972

A Great Book of Instances

Geoffrey O'Brien

There is a sequence at the end of Frederick Wiseman's *Titicut Follies* (1967)—the next to last—in which a casket is taken from a hearse and carried to a gravesite by a group of inmates of Massachusetts's Bridgewater State Hospital for the criminally insane. They are focused on their task, talking among themselves in low tones as they maneuver the casket into position. Then the priest, Father Mulligan, reads a very brief service (the inmates intoning at the appropriate moment "And let perpetual light shine upon him") concluding with: "Remember, man, that thou are dust, and unto dust thou shalt return. That's all." Priest and inmates quickly depart and for a moment the casket occupies the center of the screen. In that same frame we get a glimpse of everything absent from the rest of the film, air and vegetation and open ground. It is a quietly shocking moment in a film with many more abrasive shocks: we are forced to acknowledge death as a relief. The deceased has made a getaway—after the strip searches, the recollections of child rape, the taunting, the tube feeding, the stony isolation cells—from an almost unbearable existence.

That impression of escape attaches itself as well to the priest's ceremonial language, which (unlike what we have been hearing up until this point) bears no trace of psychiatric jargon and no distortions of mental illness. Before this, we have encountered Father Mulligan in other people's words, as the subject of a joke told at the staff-and-inmate musical show that frames the film and gives it its title, as a character in the disordered rant of the film's most talkative personage, as part of a song improvised by another inmate. We have seen him, a few moments before the cemetery scene, administering last rites. His performance of these rituals carried out countless times before seems no more than perfunctory, yet even in his fairly rushed delivery the phrase "eternal rest" acquires, in the context the film has created, a startling freshness. Here at last is language that is coherent, deliberate, profoundly meaningful, and pristinely devoid of any personal expression. And then it's back to the show: "Sing and dance and take a chance. Until another year, we're through." While guards and inmates take their curtain call, we are given, as throughout the film, constant flickers of expression and gesture hinting at more personal history than any image or any film could possibly encompass.

We are also conscious throughout of the vigor of juxtaposition, the placement of captured images to produce (here far more than in the later films) a species of found expressionism. The persistent visual impression—and shot for shot it is one of the most indelible of films, filled with moments that come back unbidden and perhaps unwanted—is often of a very old movie, surviving in fragments, some archaic shadow world emanating from a lost corner of Germany or Russia, an apparition from the realm of masks and monsters and white-faced clowns made all the more unsettling by the ghostly theatricality of pom-poms and "Strike Up the Band." The oldness has to do with Bridgewater itself conforming to our sense of an anachronistic dungeon far removed from the modernity of 1967, a place of darkness into which Wiseman has descended with camera and tape recorder in order to bring images out into the light. The present tense of documentary, of the unrehearsed moment captured live, is inflected by a sense of lag or undertow, as if the place itself annulled time.

Wiseman's first film already has the characteristics of those that followed—the absence of written captions or narration or talking-head interviews, the structural freedom permitting scenes out of chronological sequence and intercutting of apparently unrelated episodes—but stands quite distinctly apart in its mood and texture. *Titicut Follies* may be read somewhat differently now than when it first appeared. It was made at a moment when representations of madness, and the trope of the asylum as mirror of the world, pervaded the culture on many different levels, from Ken Kesey's novel *One Flew Over the Cuckoo's Nest* (1962) and Peter Weiss's play *Marat/Sade* (1963) to movies as various as Samuel Fuller's *Shock Corridor* (1963) and Philippe de Broca's *King of Hearts* (1966). This was the heyday of the antipsychiatry of R. D. Laing and David Cooper. An audience primed to see headshrinkers as oppressors had limited sympathy to spare for the psychiatric staff of Bridgewater. The episode in the yard where inmates discuss the pros and cons of the Vietnam War—at a time when similar discussions, not necessarily more cogent or better informed, could be heard in any college dorm or neighborhood bar—needed no prompting to be read as a transparent commentary on the insanity of the war itself.

Titicut Follies. 1967

Certainly *Titicut Follies* exposes horrors of callousness, casual cruelty, and myopic indifference—and relays suggestions of a decadent bureaucracy in keeping with the decayed physical condition of the hospital itself—yet its enduring power and mystery go far beyond the social impact of any such exposé. The power and mystery have everything to do with the approach Wiseman broached here and has continued to explore, the direct presentation of scenes without preparation or commentary, leaving the spectator at every point to determine what is going on and what its significance might be. In many of Wiseman's later films there is a kind of relief at the outset in not being given names and dates and arguments to frame our perception: we are allowed to come upon the world and recognize it. Calmed initially by a sense of familiarity—as if after all anything we see could only be an extension of the world we know—we are at the same time, for the same reason, nudged into a residual anxious alertness.

Throughout his work there is a sense of being permitted to see with the eyes of a child or a stranger, knowing little or nothing of where we are and what has brought us here. We have to rely on visual and aural clues that we learn to read as we once did as a matter of course, and to respond with unanticipated intimacy to people to whom we have not been introduced. We find ourselves assessing them immediately—on the basis perhaps of the most random traits, the shape of a mouth, the movement of a wrist, the style of a shirt—and, again with the child's wariness, feeling out very rapidly who will help or who will hurt, and who might give us some idea of what is going on. When people talk we listen attentively to pick up useful scraps of information or anything that sounds like helpful advice.

Such advice is hard to find in *Titicut Follies.* Any familiarity here—for most viewers—is likely to be that of a deeply rooted and unpleasant dream, the aura of a dreaded place that everyone can imagine even if they have never been there: a place either without charity or where charity does little apparent good, where one has no freedom and not even a language in which to adequately express that lack, or rather where one's way of using language for such expression becomes itself a reason for further deprivation. The more the patient Vladimir asserts his sanity the more hopeless his case becomes. Yet the more logically the psychiatrists frame their arguments, the more apparent it becomes that they have little hope to offer the patients in their charge. The chain-smoking Dr. Ross, blinking furiously as he questions a child molester or indifferently flicking ashes as he force-feeds a strapped-down inmate, might be a stone-hearted incompetent or a tragically burnt-out case, murmuring essentially to himself the answers that he knows his patients won't absorb anyway. He might even be a man whose compassion is well concealed for purposes of self-preservation in a relentlessly chaotic environment where, in Vladimir's words, "All they do is throw cups around. . . . It's noisy, they got two television sets which are blaring, machines which are going." The guards and attendants who are there to hold chaos at bay are themselves inextricably caught up in it, and can be seen as condemned to their fate as much as the inmates.

Titicut Follies conveys from the outset an overwhelming sense of transgression. I use the word "transgression" with caution, given the film's contentious legal history, merely to register the irresistible feeling for the spectator of entering a place off-limits, of being given to see what no outsider was intended to see. Although the hospital is a place of torment, whether by forces external or internal, not everything we see is appalling. But the marginally brighter bits—the birthday party with the trio singing "Have You Ever Been Lonely?";

the guard Eddie with his energetic clowning; the kindly volunteer ladies; the nurse moved by her letter from an inmate ("When you get a letter like this . . . it makes you feel as though, well, you at least tried")—tend to be overshadowed by, notably, the scene early on in which the inmate Jim is taunted by the guards ("You gonna keep that room clean, Jim?") until he explodes in rage. The moments that follow—Jim, naked, stamping up and down in his cell, beating on the barred window—bring us as near as we can be brought into the unreachable space of someone else's locked-in solitude. The shot in which Jim stares toward the camera acknowledges the insuperability of the barrier. We are here beyond any easy question of moral meaning, and well beyond the limits of a notion of privacy that would prevent such a scene ever from being seen. A line has been crossed, and all of Wiseman's work might be seen as a continuing exploration of the implications of that crossing.

Titicut Follies captures with exactness how unbearable the progression from one moment to the next can become for those without occupation. The doors that close on the inmates lock them into spaces designed for nothing to happen in them. Wiseman's subsequent films are so much about keeping busy: sometimes usefully, sometimes in fulfillment of an obscure and perhaps incomprehensible obligation, the people are all, monks or janitors or security guards or missile-launch instructors, working on something. The inmates in *Titicut Follies* are precisely those with nothing to do except somehow get better in a place and under conditions where, it seems, few are likely to. "Why you keeping a man from work?" an African-American inmate protests. (A guard asks him if he wants to sell watermelons.) "*Where* can I work? I'd like to know where can I work?" The smallest task fulfilled becomes the minimum definition of a bearable life, even if the task is only to remember the lyrics of "Chinatown, My Chinatown."

Contemplation of the nature of a task and the purpose for which separate tasks converge is a continuing thread in Wiseman's work, as one system after another passes in review. In the process his work as a whole becomes a lexicon of the world. It could be cross-referenced by means of analogous components that repeat from film to film—machines, songs, television programs, animals, priests, janitors, documents, hairstyles—and indexed to serve as a guide to modes of human interaction: a great book of instances. What all those instances would add up to, in any

given film and in the work as a whole, remains very much an open question. To keep the question open seems to be the constantly reiterated premise, a premise often underscored by the people he films. "Life is rushing by and sometimes we wonder whether we grasp its meaning," says a priest in *Racetrack* (1985). "Why do some people live? What is his aim in life?" asks a neighbor in *Law and Order* (1969) as she watches a wino being rousted from the pavement by a couple of policemen.

These are films in which we have emerged from the underworld of *Titicut Follies*, even if the difference is not always obvious. The world above ground can seem as much of a prison house, as we enter environments that overlap with the imaginative worlds of such postmodern paranoid systems analysts as Gaddis, Mailer, Pynchon, Kubrick. Wiseman's work is, precisely, pared of their exaggeration and caricature, pared likewise of special pleading; but that does not necessarily make it less terrifying. It would not be hard to read *Welfare* (1975) in the light of absurdism—and in case the point were missed, one of the welfare clients, Mr. Hirsch, is there to emphasize it, in a speech that might have been written for a play of his own devising: "I've been waiting for the last hundred-and-twenty-four days since I got out of the hospital, waiting for something—Godot. But you know what happens, you know what happens in the story of Godot. He never came."

What better arena than the welfare system for an exposition of the madness of bureaucracy, the entrapment of hapless individuals, both clients and workers, in an endless round of interviews and paper shuffling, the sense of a just adjudication perpetually deferred. That exposition is made in full, yet such a description would give little idea of the actual character of *Welfare*, a film which finds extraordinarily diverse life in the interstices of boredom and obfuscation and maddening frustration. For me it is the great movie about New York in the 1970s, a great tragicomedy of need and deception and resignation and, above all, ceaseless and vigorous argument. Everybody works to make sense of things at every moment, often under extreme pressure.

The disparate episodes spill over with the contradictory meanings imparted to them by their participants. The hapless Mrs. Johnson, trying to cut through walls of red tape, being finally unforgettably counseled by another client, "Valerie, Valerie, Valerie, Valerie, Valerie. You not going to get nowhere up here arguing with him. . . . Baby, he only got a certain amount of authority"; the

bored young black policeman amusing himself by debating at extraordinary length with a racist mugging victim; the complex multiple confrontation, a staggering instance of a mise-en-scène not so much imposed as discovered, of a client, her daughter, an unsympathetic welfare worker, a policeman, and a supervisor: to summarize all that is going on in any one of these scenes would be the work of many pages, a whole volume perhaps, and no two observers would agree on what had been observed.

One does not need to have applied for welfare or to have worked for the welfare system to have inhabited some part of this world. We have some knowledge of these benches, these forms, these ritualized question-and-answer sessions, these evasions and confrontations. Even if, say, I only applied for unemployment insurance, or worked in an office where low-level employees were routinely subjected to lie-detector tests, or made photocopies in a shop where just such exhausted people made multiple copies of endlessly refolded official documents, *Welfare* provokes an almost overwhelming sense of immersion in a remembered place.

The power of memory is often called into play by Wiseman's films. One is constantly jogged into a comparison with other instances, other places, other people, and that recognition enlists us into an active participation. You share a space with what is on the screen, as if you were watching, in Gertrude Stein's phrase, everybody's autobiography. Whatever system is on display is never more than a further reach of the one you inhabit. The absence of narration elicits the spectator's own commentary, which becomes part of the film: a provisional working out of where one is in relation to each moment as it passes. You are not only given the opportunity to imagine yourself variously in each role (on both sides of the desk, for instance, in *Welfare*) but can hardly evade that responsibility, and in the process are forced to recognize your own limits and biases. A constant exercise in definition is enforced. You might come to feel uncannily as if the film were looking back at you, taking note of your response to it; and to feel that, after inhabiting it for two or three hours, it had ended by inhabiting you.

In *Titicut Follies* and *Welfare*, as in the rest of Wiseman's films, there is never any pretense that what we see constitutes the main or only story. On the contrary we are thoroughly aware that other scenes could have been shown, that a nearly infinite number of other films could have emerged from within the selected field. The filmmaker exercises the choice of what to look at and how long to sustain that gaze, and in doing so makes us fully conscious of the power inherent in that choice. We are invited to think about the logic of the structures he establishes. The cutting is the (supposedly absent) commentary just as it is the governor of rhythm and duration and narrative form. The films are as much meditations on editing as on what is edited. It is not the least of their genius to have made palpable—indeed breathlessly involving—the notion of film editing as an existential decision.

Welfare. 1975

Hospital. 1969

Near Death / Near Life

Jay Neugeboren

The scene seems, at first, chilling. Mister C., a thirty-three-year-old man, has died, leaving behind a wife and three young children. We have come to know the wife, have met the children (ages twelve, nine, five), and have watched for more than an hour, screen-time, while Mister C.'s wife, doctors, and nurses try to figure out why things have gone bad so suddenly, and what, if anything, can be done to save Mister C.'s life and, if nothing can be done, how to manage his final hours. A moment after we watch nurses wrap Mister C.'s body in sheets, transfer it from bed to gurney, walk it along corridors and in and out of elevators, and slide it into a locker in the hospital's morgue, we hear the voice of the young doctor who has been caring for Mister C. The doctor is summarizing Mister C.'s case for several dozen doctors, nurses, and medical students in a crowded room, some students standing on risers (or chairs), straining to get a better view of what we see next: Mister C.'s internal organs laid out neatly on a metal tray as if in a butcher shop.

We see close-ups of organs and parts of organs, and we see staff members pick them up, pat them down, palpate them, turn them over, and then, at closer range—the tray fills the screen—we see gloved hands handling the organs while a doctor tells us that looking at the lungs, you wouldn't be aware of how fibrotic they are, but if you touch them, as many now do, you'd see that they're of a "very woody consistency."

The scene takes place near the end of the fourth hour of Frederick Wiseman's remarkable six-hour film, *Near Death*, during which we live with patients, patients' families, and staff on the intensive care unit of Beth Israel hospital in Boston. The year is 1989, and in the hours preceding Mister C.'s death, we have been witness to all that medical technology can offer to the dying by way of treatment and comfort, and we have been immersed—drenched, really—in the complexity of decisions that doctors, nurses, and family members make during what are, usually, the last days and hours of a loved one's life. We have seen doctors and nurses debate courses of action and lay out medical realities and choices; we have seen family members confer, worry, and grieve; and we have seen patients die. By the time we see Mister C.'s internal organs, we are no longer

Near Death. 1989

strangers to the human body and all it can be subjected to when in a state of final deterioration.

Still, the abrupt shift from living with a man we have come to know to seeing his internal organs displayed and probed is, at first, shocking—a seemingly cold disregard for the man's humanity ("Okay," the pathologist says at the scene's end, as Mister C.'s organs are covered with a cloth, "why don't we do the next"). The essence of the scene, however, is not callousness, but kindness. When Mister C.'s doctor reports that Mister C. died at about five o'clock the evening before, he adds that the wife said that if there were anything that could be learned from her husband's illness and death, that's what he would want, and that's what she wants.

Steadily and ruthlessly, the film raises questions: What can we learn about illness, disease, and death by watching, closely, how we tend to the dying? What do we know about why and how people become ill and die? What is the responsibility of doctors (and families)? And, by implication, as in the two other Wiseman films set in hospitals—*Titicut Follies* (1967) and *Hospital* (1969)—what is our collective (societal) responsibility to those who are helpless to help themselves?

One way of understanding the complex of issues that are the ongoing substance of these films—films that may, at times, seem leisurely, even casual in their attention to any one moment—is to see that by giving us stories of people in crisis who are dependent upon others for their well-being and survival, the films also ask us to try to understand where, in such moments and lives, the sources of kindness and of hope (and of their opposites) may lie.

Despite a dedicated, well-trained staff, there are no good outcomes here; virtually all the patients we meet in *Near Death* die. Again and again, and with exquisite consideration for patient and family members, doctors and nurses say the same things: that they have "no explanation" for why a patient has taken a turn for the worse; that they have better and more powerful technologies than ever, yet the benefits to patients are unclear, and meaningful recoveries extremely rare; that after years of work they wonder if they have been of *any* help to *anyone*; that their work may, in essence, be "nihilistic"—that they may, as one doctor puts it, be nothing more than furniture salesmen offering families meaningless options.

I can tell you I can do things to let you live for six months instead of three, one doctor says to another, but will I also say how god-awful those three extra months will be? That your mouth will be so raw you won't be able to eat, that you'll be in constant pain, that you'll be on and off life support machines, and in and out of the ICU? There's this too, the other doctor says: if the patient chooses three months, how much better, if at all, will *those* months be?

Nurses and doctors argue about how much information to provide, about what constitutes a "well-informed decision," about the degree to which the way a doctor presents options *manipulates* the decision a family or a patient makes, about whether a family should be asked to make decisions it's not competent to make, and about the extent to which doctors and nurses bring their own values—about God, life, death, medicine, and quality of life—to a case.

For large segments of *Near Death*, we may see nothing other than a patient lying in a bed, tubes going in and out of head and body, or we may attend conversations between a doctor or nurse and a family member. These conversations go on at length, in closed and narrow spaces—most often a hospital corridor—and repeat previous conversations: Should we resuscitate or not? Should we let the patient breathe on his or her own? Should we pursue *everything* medicine can do, which may involve treatments closer to torture than to palliative care, or should we, instead, do what we can to make the patient *comfortable* (i.e., put in a morphine drip until the patient expires)? Though the staff is relentlessly thoughtful, we may wonder at times: are they, for all their skill and compassion, killing with kindness? What, after all, would it be like to lie immobile in a bed, unable to talk, your face covered with tape, tubes and drips running in and out of your body, while doctors ask *you* to approve or reject forms of treatment that may, perhaps within minutes, lead to your death?

"There's a certain grain of stupidity that the writer of fiction can hardly do without, and this is the quality of having to stare, of not getting the point at once," Flannery O'Connor has written. "The longer you look at one object, the more of the world you see in it; and it's well to remember that the serious fiction writer always writes about the whole world, no matter how limited his particular scene. For him, the bomb that was dropped on Hiroshima affects life on the Oconee River, and there's not anything he can do about it."[1]

So it is with Frederick Wiseman. His camera won't stop staring at its subjects, and it touches everything it sees with a tenderness that is anything but innocent. Wiseman disparages the notion that his films are cinéma vérité, which to him "connotes just hanging around with one thing being as valuable as another." He takes rightful pride in reducing hundreds of hours of shooting to a carefully sequenced few hours of film. Although his films are based on "un-staged, un-manipulated actions," the editing "is highly manipulative and the shooting is highly manipulative."[2]

Wiseman pays close attention to the intricacies of moments by lingering, for example, on a glass of milk resting on a table next to a dying patient's bed, and on the way a slant of light bathes the glass and makes of it a Vermeer-like still-life; or by pausing on a man in bed, his face covered in bandages, his body attached to multiple monitors and IV lines, and making of him, in the stillness of his repose and imminent death, an ineffable combination of beauty and pathos.

Through thousands of choices of what to show and, at least as important, of what *not* to show (we see nothing, for example, of the staff, family, or patients beyond their time on the ICU), and by patiently staring at people in a particular moment of their lives, Wiseman makes us acutely aware of the mystery of our mortality—of how and why we die when we do—while also asking us to be aware of the larger world, markedly absent in the film, that exists beyond the hospital. And, as with Mister C.'s organs, he calls attention to how generous we sometimes are when we suffer loss in trying to delay or prevent loss for others.

Although *Near Death* is a movie in which death is omnipresent and hope rarely rewarded, it is an antidote to the two other Wiseman films set in hospitals. *Titicut Follies*, about mental patients incarcerated in the Bridgewater, Massachusetts, state hospital for the criminally insane, is very much about the living, and is suffused with a sense of just how hopeless and cruel life can be. Patients live in locked cells that are without lights, sinks, toilets, or beds; they are herded around naked while being prodded and taunted by guards; and they are chemically lobotomized with drugs. In one scene a man lies on a table in a busy, dingy room, his legs and arms held down with twisted towels by four guards while a doctor shoves a long tube into his nose and pours in a liquid nutrient as if pouring oil into a car engine. The doctor smokes and jokes with the guards all the while, the ash from his cigarette ever longer and threatening to fall into the nutrient.

We cut back and forth from this scene to shots of the same patient being shaved, only to realize after a short while that the patient is being shaved because he is dead. The mortician who tends to him is one of the few people in the film who show any kindness toward a patient. And a scene in which a priest bestows last rites on another patient is the only scene in which a patient lies on a real bed, a real pillow under his head. The very freshness and whiteness of the pillowcase, in this landscape of misery, startles.

The emergency room in *Hospital* is full of hundreds of people waiting for doctors, but if we didn't know we were in a hospital (the Metropolitan Hospital in New York), the room would seem a dilapidated, crowded bus station—an urban purgatory in a city beyond repair or redemption. We meet abandoned children, lifeless drug addicts, frightened old men, lonely old women; we watch surgery take place in dimly lit rooms, and see doctors plead with bureaucrats, by phone, for the wherewithal to do their work. One doctor declares the conditions of a woman's transfer "absurd." There were no notes or data accompanying her from the hospital that transferred her, and her life, by these over-sights, has been put into jeopardy. The doctor is beyond despair, and after haranguing what may be an answering machine, he notes, coolly, that this happens all the time and whenever it happens he makes it a point to call the hospital administrator and register his complaint.

In *Near Death*, as in certain Dutch paintings of interiors (living rooms warmly furnished and kitchens full of food, rooms from which we look through windows to see calm, gray seas and ships set to sail), we often look past the backlit silhouettes of staff and family to see, through large hospital windows, the city of Boston in full, midday light.

In *Hospital* we live in dark rooms and corridors, never see out a window, never glimpse the world beyond the hospital. As Joseph Morgenstern has written: "The moral is clear. Do not be poor in this land of untold riches: if you are poor, do not be sick."[3] By rapid cuts, and attention to overtly repulsive detail (an addict vomiting profusely and repeatedly, a stomach being sliced open), here, as in *Titicut Follies*, Wiseman calls attention not merely to the harshness, violence, and helplessness endemic to the lives of the poor and the mad, but to the absence in their lives of anything resembling compassion.

In 1967, at a time when Wiseman was filming *Titicut Follies*, my brother Robert was incarcerated at Creedmoor State Hospital for the Insane in New York City. He lived at Creedmoor, on and off, with several thousand other patients (the D building had one doctor for six hundred patients) for four and a half years, during which time he was heavily medicated, straitjacketed, subjected to insulin shock therapy, beaten up, and intermittently paraded before tribunal-like "review boards" which interrogated him to determine if and when he might be fit for discharge.

In *Titicut Follies*, an articulate young man, sent to Bridgewater for "observation" a year and a half before, asks a review board: "How can I improve if I'm getting worse?" ("How can I become sane," Robert would ask, "if I'm surrounded by insane people?" Or, pleading with me to get him out: "Don't you see, Jay, I'm sane—that's why I'm here—I'm *in* sane!")

The name of the game at Bridgewater, as it was at Creedmoor and other state hospitals I've visited, is crowd control and humiliation. When the Bridgewater patient is forcibly taken away ("I need peace and quiet," he says calmly, "and this place is disturbing me"), the board's psychiatrist recommends higher doses of tranquilizers; when my brother became irritable or belligerent, his

medications were increased and he was placed on isolation: living twenty-four hours a day in a bare room. His doctors called this "reduced stimulation."

Whether a patient, forty years ago, walks around naked while guards jeer at him—or whether my brother, one year ago, requesting kosher food, is shouted at by a psychiatrist ("Stop talking like a lunatic!")—the effect is the same: to close them down and shut them up, and thereby deprive them of anything resembling an identity other than that of a madman.

Our mother was a registered nurse—an exceptionally beautiful, capable woman (first in her nursing school class at Jamaica Hospital in Queens, New York), beloved of doctors and patients. She often worked double shifts in order to support our family, yet I saw her only in her life *outside* hospitals, and while I watched Wiseman's films, I kept wishing he and his 16mm camera had been there a half-century ago, filming her while she worked so I could see what she was like when she conferred with doctors, assisted in surgery, or tended to patients. I kept wishing he could have been with me in our small apartment in Brooklyn when, at six or seven years old, I would be given the privilege of shining her nursing shoes. While she slept, I would sit on the floor just outside our bathroom, newspaper spread out under me while I dipped an applicator in and out of a container of shoe polish and carefully swabbed on the creamy white liquid. After the shoes dried, I placed them next to her bedroom door, so they would be there for her when she woke in the morning and got ready to leave for work.

These were peaceful, happy moments in a sometimes grim childhood, and were Wiseman there what he might have noticed was that, in these moments, I was able to feel a kind of tenderness that he himself must know when, by touching people and objects, he and his camera find small, bright moments of hope in an ordinarily cruel and dark world.

1. Flannery O'Connor, "The Nature and Aim of Fiction," in *Mystery and Manners: Occasional Prose*, ed. Sally and Robert Fitzgerald (New York: Farrar, Straus, and Giroux, 1969), p. 77.

2. Frederick Wiseman, interview by Kaleem Aftab and Alexandra Weltz, *Film West* 40, http://www.iol.ie/-galfilm/filmwest/40wiseman.htm.

3. Joseph Morgenstern, "It Don't Make Sense," *Newsweek* 75, no. 6 (February 9, 1970): 85.

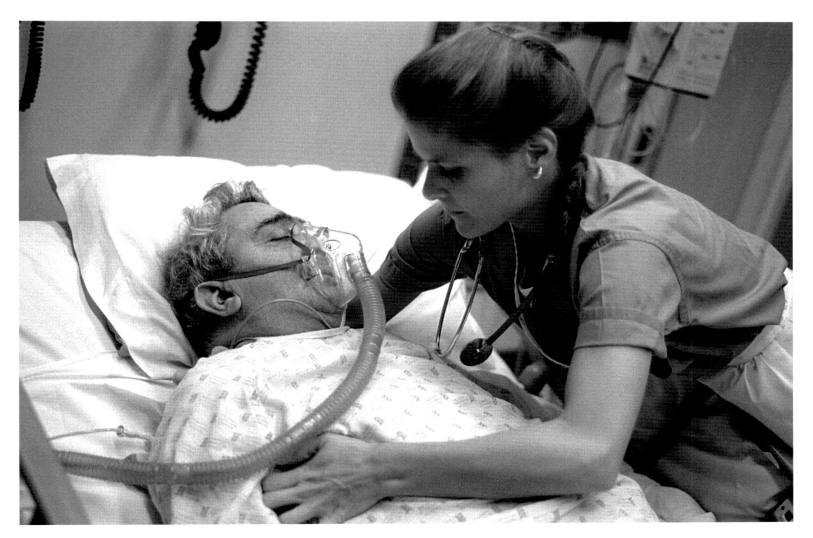

Near Death. 1989

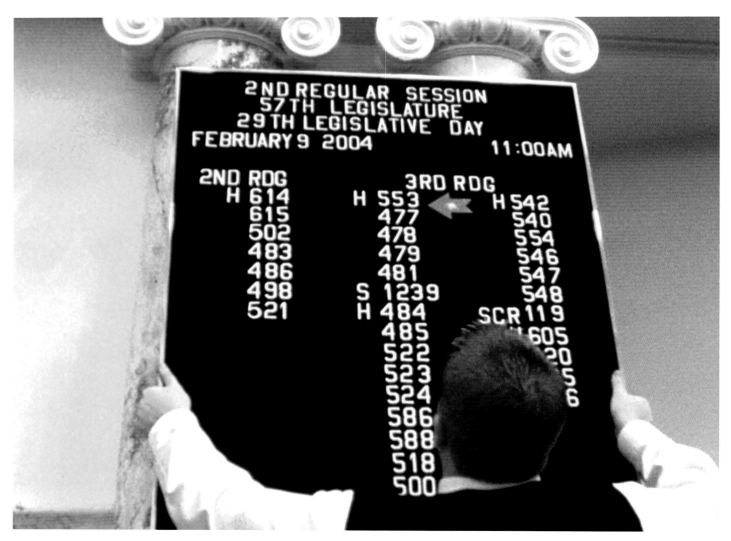

State Legislature. 2006

The Ties That Bind

Pierre Legendre

What makes a work possible is its author's capacity to be a resistant. By that I mean: to have worked in solitude and experienced opposition, muted or violent, to finally get a hold on what he is, a craftsman clinging to the task of fashioning, practicing, and instructing those who come to him. And I am less impressed by the flood of praise belatedly bestowed on Frederick Wiseman than by the laxness of most of the commentaries, in France at least, on the issue at hand with his films: that he has created a cinema of the institution.

The complete decline of a sense of what is important is not unrelated to this observation. We live in a time of disorientation. The leveling of thought, the race toward flashy and ephemeral formulations, a vague desire to bring critique to plebiscitary practices—none of this favors investigating the lesson of a body of work that is certainly unfinished and has a rich future before it, but that has long had its own goals in sight. What is there that is essential about Frederick Wiseman, essen-tial to the very meaning of cinema, the cinematographic principle?

It should be noted that Wiseman began as a law-yer, more specifically a professor of law. Is that why I sense his willingness to approach social monuments as blocks of fiction, sufficient in and of themselves, posited there as enigmas, equal to things we call Nature? When I met him for the first time, I understood that behind his laughter and humor, he was almost apologetic; I knew he had hesitations. Wiseman is one of those people who, educated in the rigor of legal architecture, has learned that one does not slip into the habitat of modern nations that easily. Those places are theaters, in accord with the political orchestra, with modern figures of the ancient Despot; this is where the drama of the subjection of man to man unfolds, farce and tragedy both, with a rigor compared since Aristotle to the logic of the hive; and no one can transgress his role or play the part of another. To dare to bring a camera here forces one to overcome the paradox of being there and being absent; it is to con-struct, in the old expression of Roman jurists, a *position*, the right position in public space, a position that usurps neither the place of the actors in question nor that of the absolute gaze—the sovereign gaze, God or the State, in a style more in keeping with the imperium of current beliefs, Society.

The *rightness* of Wiseman comes from his refusal to claim to do more than the actor who, like a miniaturist in a copyist's studio, comes to add his iconographic transcription, his interpretation of the social text to the text—to the text that is what it is—between the lines or in the margins, in this case by means of the cinema. If this notation indeed describes the position of a filmmaker of the institution, it is because Wiseman has been compelled to make work without embellishment, in order to be truthful. Nowadays, this asceticism of discourse is rather rare. With Wiseman we are far from those artificial geniuses who declaim on the power of the bad guys and make a career out of being outraged, talking heads who inundate us with their states of mind.

One more term, to prepare the ground; I borrow it from the legal vocabulary: "authentication." It seems to me to describe each film very opportunely. Wiseman's work is not a conglomeration of anecdotes; it looks at life at the second level of truth, where discourses are marked, passed though the filter of the camera. The camera, in short, acts as a stamp that certifies the situations of discourse, for example the expressions and gestures of professional life through which an institution, whatever it may be, are expressed with the truth of a flesh-and-blood person. In our contemporary, media-driven society, a cinema of the institution authenticates the topic at hand for all to see, namely this: the social and political fiction that speaks through the mouth of those who bring it to life and from this institutional mirage fashion their own lives.

Of course, this cinema is not accessible to scientists, to the brilliant minds of today, to the positivist set that does not suspect questions of editing and theatricality, without which the banality would be deprived of meaning. Wiseman's films are comprehensible only to those who feel the truth of the masks, the intensity of scraps of conversation between ordinary interlocutors, the snippets of intrigue and comedy that are at the heart of things in the everyday experience of the premises, wherever they may be. The innocence of the unremarkable emerges as an enigma and becomes the material of a genre. And it is precisely this—the unveiling of what is most common—that makes these documentaries an absolutely particular type of film. I would say, as with opera, one enters it or does not enter it; it requires a belief in something other than what one sees.

What Sort of Belief Sustains Wiseman's Cinema?

What belief? Let's be clear. This is not a matter of determining the opinion of the maker of *Near Death* (1989) on American democracy as transposed in therapeutic decision-making in the terminal phase, or of *Juvenile Court* (1973) on justice for minors, the function of the judge and expert committees, and who knows what else. Wiseman's political thoughts do not interest me; they would bore me as much as the endless mediacentric discourse that deplores the perpetual crisis of society and the sorrows of our time. I am not asking questions in the style of the social novel, or of sociological inquiry. No, that's not it. I'm trying to pinpoint another reason to work with the camera besides expressing an opinion (an easy game of which we've had our fill). I'm trying to understand the idea at the core of this filmmaker's works, in connection with the way in which man is fabricated, the way in which he walks toward a destiny, and also the way in which he breaks down. What idea does this cinema have of the human machinery, of this machinery of words? And why put this idea into film? This, for me, is the horizon of belief at work in the documentary, supported, as Wiseman says himself, by an "intense look at a specific reality"—at a particular segment of humanity, filmed in a particular institutional situation. At that point what face of truth comes to us, through the mirror of the screen?

I will offer here a general remark. The works of an artist, like every production of the mind, no longer belong to him, and the explanations he gives of them are to be put into perspective. An oeuvre worthy of the name, a great oeuvre—by which I mean, one that moves forward from an initial question, develops its erudition, and tends toward a constantly receding point of com-

Domestic Violence 2. 2002

pletion—escapes its maker, because the most human aspects of what he is saying exceed him. When Wiseman says he wants "to show how people live today," or that "what interests me is bringing a critical eye to what happens in different places," he says nothing that might enlighten us, or enlighten himself, about what he is doing. He is just summarizing what he knows about what he does for those who ask him: I work, and I work as a critic. In other words, literally, my work consists of judging, of choosing what is decisive.

If this is indeed the message, it is now up to us to see it—we might even say to judge and to choose for ourselves. As viewers, we enter the filmmaker's discourse from a remove, and he, in a way, finds himself displaced. The time has come for commentary. Privilege and distance allow a third eye. Consequently, the work may take the shape and assume the rigor of instruction, through a placing into perspective that reveals a trajectory, highlights an initial position, outlines a few strong points in the arduous repetition of a central theme. Now I can express what I see.

I see *Titicut Follies* (1967) as the way in to Wiseman, and *Model* (1980) as the cutting edge of his work. Between these two ends, I see an obvious, rich expansion of side routes but ones that reprise and punctuate this latent theme, always veiled by the comings and goings of the occupants of the scene: the omnipresent institution, a stringing up of a humanity of marionettes under the discordant heading of, to borrow the title of another of his films, "Law and Order."

Marionettes, is that right? Yes, provided we recall the classical discourse of the West on the human being grappling with his condition—connected by artificial ties to Power with a capital *P*, to the enigmatic assemblage of the social theater, to the puller of strings that haunts the speaking species. In *Model*, a young woman asks whether her tableau will be like a still life. In another passage, the model is told: "The whole reason you're going out to work [for] the photographers is to see what your limits are." The quintessence of the question facing mankind in Wiseman's films is contained in these startling formulations, which come not from Mount Olympus but from the depths of everyday banality.

Let us return to the initial question, which is the way in to Wiseman, *Titicut Follies*, a requisite reference point for any commentator. It is the initial question in the sense that the author, formerly a professor of criminal law, put his finger on the source of all institutional scaffolding, while encountering Crime and Madness, locked up behind the walls of Bridgewater, a state psychiatric prison in Massachusetts. Whether he is conscious of this source doesn't matter too much, because the idea was not to construct the narrative of a sort of camp—yet another one—with its lot of sorrow, ennui, and imbecility, but to agree to be confronted, he as a filmmaker and we along with him, with the most dramatic elements of the human condition, with the unexpected separation of man from himself, which is to say the collapse of the principle of Reason. In the confines of the world of the living, this is the hell of the living dead, a prison/asylum where guards and doctors, our spokespeople, hate the madness in front of them and their own fear of it. The creation of institutions, on a scale of systems shared by the planet in all places at all times, consists of this: the ordering of the relationship between the individual and the authority of Reason. *Titicut Follies*, Wiseman's first work, affects us so strongly because we are very aware that the discourse of Reason and Madness is in fact the discourse of fear, and that in our century it has become the quintessential weapon of tyrannies.

Yet it seems to me that *Titicut Follies* might also encourage us to consider an intellectual impasse of ultramodern societies of the West: their inability to tackle the problem of Reason other than in terms of individual reason, based on increasingly medicalized standards these days. On first viewing, I immediately compared this document with Jean Rouch's film, *Les Maîtres fous* (*The Mad Masters*, 1955), which proves the gulf that separates us—rationalists formed by the hermeticism of discourse—from a problematization of the principle of Reason more open to inquiry into the corridors of our own rationality. What we do not understand is the very concept of Reason and the amalgam it forms with the concept of the Institution. Now, the Institution is nothing other than the human being's technique of assembling himself, the image he has of himself—a technique thanks to which the individual (that is, each of us) can support the repertoire with a role, can play a part in this theater of masks that we call Society. To institute Reason is to construct a theater of images. Now it remains to be seen who the Master in this theater, the puller of the strings, is and why a game like this is so dramatic. Of the room to maneuver that is allotted to the individual, Wiseman speaks with precision and the same rightness in a film that I consider his apogee, his cutting edge, as I said: *Model*.

Model. 1980

In the course of doing my work of analysis and comparison—a private festival in which I select and crown what is known as "auteur cinema"—I give *Model* first prize. First, for its form. Composition such as this—beginning with the compositions created in advertising agencies by the designers, makeup artists, scriptwriters, and photographers of the sort who gravitate toward models who have been deified—has something demiurgic about it. This battle for the image has to do with the quest for the absolute, sessions of cool seduction affecting the iconological pose; the professionalism of love photographed—an example being the couple captured in front of American flags—joins the religious metaphysics of emblems, this European Baroque discourse that presupposed the Divine Hand. To manage to get the viewer to participate in the work of repetition and posing, to inscribe our own gaze in the wonderful *tableaux vivants*, to suggest, finally, that we are witnessing scenes of rapture captured by the camera like a liturgical celebration, is great art. An art that knows how to use the slag of preparatory gestures and make them the gestures of an actor or painter, an art that transforms the racket of a passing car into a wrenching human cry. We see, through maps of New York, the extent to which the urban order

in Manhattan, a seeming jungle of buildings, streets, common spaces, and bridges, can produce effects of nature. Nature is there, violent, unexpected, and seemingly immutable. *Model*, the film, is itself constructed, as precise and beautiful as the models it displays. A cult of form without formalism, a selective documentary work that handles with discretion the capacity to show; the opposite, then, of catchall expressionism, which nowadays is doing quite well.

Should I venture to discern the social contents and subjective value of what is said by all these random actors? I mean: to interpret the interpretation, this repertoire that *Model* mediatizes. Enclosed in institutionalized representations, man inhabits a discourse and speaks of what he sees. Through this film, we watch the live fabrication of a mirror held out to each individual in ultramodern culture, a mirror built to teach man how to resemble. An advertising agency—a machine that manufactures the truth of the image of things—reveals the process of editing, which consists of veiling the world and human beings, in order to make them familiar, desirable, close.

What do the seriousness, dedication, and meticulousness of the models teach us? What does the docility of the model, male or female, eager to repeat the pose, under the absolute and indisputable yoke of a fashion director or photographer, teach us? And the women, above all, trained to become these large, magical animals, paintings or sculptures that are living yet illusory like trompe l'oeil? I will borrow a term from Alciat, scholar of the Renaissance and theoretician of emblems: *veritas falsa* (false truth). That is what the advertising industry teaches. Seeing the film, a militant partisan of the *true truth*, a sociologist of the woman-as-object, protested that they let themselves be treated like lapdogs; he believed he saw tyranny. That person knows nothing of the love of images, or the artificiality of human desire, or the rhetorical passion behind which the torment of existing is sheltered.

Throughout the film, I was struck by statements addressed to the models suggesting they must project themselves in a certain way. Such statements represent the depths of the uncertainty with which we are all confronted if only we remember our childhoods. The agency Wiseman filmed—a theatrical institution redoubled—is an archetypal place, where some of the great contemporary symbols are organized; a place of truth, then, because the height of artifice is also the height of sincerity.

The Cinematographic Principle According to Wiseman

If, on the level I am investigating, I have followed not so much Wiseman's intentions as his remarks after the fact (after this or that presentation of his work) and above all the tangible result of his undertaking over time, it is to show that the stars of his films are the institutions, the standardized places of discourse. The belief which sustains this *basic cinema*, if I may describe it that way, could be summed up very simply: man dramatically inhabits everyday life, normality, and the subject's room to maneuver—the subject declared free by political constitutions—is so deficient that we have to doubt the pertinence of the term "individual." I would add that the human being is grappling with his status as a marionette: a notion to consider, not in the sense of the vulgar instrumentation of modern propaganda, but from the ancient perspective of the logical animal prey to the strife of his being. This cinema reminds me of the words of Ernst Jünger—author of the famous work *Der Arbeiter* (*The Worker*, 1932), which described the man of the masses—because it is in fact a matter of understanding, through what we are experiencing, "the essential and ineluctable membership to the type, like a form, a reproduction of the Figure, which is achieved under the constraint of an iron law."[1] Which amounts to saying, as Jünger did, that the famous "individual" is not irreplaceable but replaceable, and that his lived experience is not unique but univocal. What does Wiseman do if not express the truth of this experience in the irrefutable mode of the quotidian as transfigured by the generalization of the camera, namely, the incredible proportions of the demands made on human beings in the hyperindustrial era by contemporary systems of inclusion (another of Jünger's terms)? What does Wiseman do if not show the emptiness in which the rebellions of suffering, the pleasures of satisfied conformism, and the typical passion for efficiency resonate these days? With great certainty and without unnecessary commiseration, Wiseman once said, in an interview, that the paradigm of the mass ideal, the new figure of normality, everything that is not *Titicut Follies* and that is so explicitly highlighted in school (*High School* [1968]) and the army (*Basic Training* [1971]), is "following others"; with the key being the inexhaustible repetition, in a democratic context, of the bond of obedience: "to be a man is to do what you are told."

The particular relief of these films today has to do with the fact that they are a denial addressed to triumphant positivist ideology, to the scientistic refrains about the abolishment of the breakdown of man. In our societies, which proclaim the inclusion of everyone as subjects of happiness, it has become simple to no longer exist, to die cheerfully, to disinhabit language. What becomes of the being of language, the separation of words and things, the "Je est un autre" of Rimbaud? Soon the word will no longer be the weapon of the species; it is getting dull, degenerating into verbose manifestations. With this one must contrast the sense of strangeness, the enigmatic rigor of what the veil of words lets us guess at, the confinement of the subject in his image, manipulated by systems of institutions in the name of a representation of the world. Therein lies the massive difficulty, to have to live as a social being in order to be present to oneself. We now have to wonder: what is living? And society no longer seems an obvious concept. Then a difficulty arises, in knowing, as Wiseman formulated it when discussing *Essene* (1972), his film on Benedictine monks, "what makes up a community . . . even when it is only made up of twenty members, as it is here." Indeed, the question is not a matter of quantity, but of an understanding of what creates a bond, a human bond.

I am tempted to transpose Diderot's remark in his *Lettre sur les aveugles* (*Letter on the Blind*, 1749), in which he spoke of a famous blind man of his time, who, he says, "saw by means of his skin. . . . Thus the blind have likewise a painting, in which their own skin serves as a canvas."[2] I say that in the age of scientism, thought—the kind that makes life, because it takes a human approach to inquiry—is offered haltingly; it expresses itself through the arts. I have more trust in Magritte questioning the foundations of mankind than in philosophy as it has become—chatter known as postmodernism, a discourse of the rear guard—and I give credit to Wiseman, who philosophizes in the dark, as Diderot would say. It is on the screen, "reading" *Basic Training* and *Essene*, that I recognize the great institutional models studied by Freud, those pillars of Western culture: the Army and the Church.

What is there to decode or decipher that is new, proposed by these monumental texts that our tired eyes can no longer even perceive and that Wiseman precisely presents for a freer questioning? Free, which is to say, unfastened from the received idea according to which a society is an amalgam of individuals, a sum total of millions, one + one + one . . . managed ad infinitum. We are invited to rediscover—I am using his words—the role of law as an organizing principle.

And we indeed rediscover—in the age of the repression of meditation through quantifiable thought—the traditional isolate, essential to every civilization, of places that cultivate law for law's sake, rules for rules' sake. Wiseman again: "What interests the army is creating soldiers, and they apply rules for that. What interests the school is a certain form of schooling with certain rules. But the occupants of the monastery are interested in the rules themselves." This makes the film *Essene* (which asks, Why the organization?) the respondent to the film *Model* (which asks, How can one be a subject?); these two films, in opposition to each other, situate the enigmatic work of composition that we call man as an intersection of two planes, thanks to which man manages to resemble man: the celebration of law and the celebration of the image of oneself. To be interested in rules for rules' sake, law for law's sake, is to be interested in the reflection for itself; it is to make the mirror, and consequently and gradually, make available to the human being the love of his own image. All societies pass through this, on parallel paths, distanced from each other and disparate but, on the dark stage where dreams are fomented and desire is ordered—the other scene, as Freud said, the unconscious scene—to converge and meet again. Still, in order to grasp the role of law as an organizing principle of both society and the subject, we

Basic Training. 1971

need an art of showing and revealing that can hesitate, use detours, walk blindly, in order to make the truth felt, that is, to guide the viewer toward thought. Or, toward what T. S. Eliot called the "sensuous apprehension of thought."[3] This is what the cinema of Wiseman is about.

Thus, the question of what establishes law for man—the institutional imperative—is constantly inscribed in and traverses all of Wiseman's films. What is the cinematographic principle, as treated by this auteur? I would say the theological and philosophical formula invented by Western antiquity: *to see the principle*. That is, what does it mean to make a film, according to Wiseman? It is a question of following an idea, the big idea that supports a work, by means of a camera. The intelligence of this instrument is in the service of a certain gaze, the orientation of the shots. The camera sees and shows, where necessary, what is right, based on the big idea.

Now, it seems to me that, without his knowing it, in the most natural way, Wiseman has said and said very well, with dazzling clarity, what he saw as the principle. In an interview, I read: "It's a thing that unites my films, this gulf that makes it so that an individual is cut off by what separates ideology from practice. Every institution is, in a sense, a microcosm of the failure of the functioning of the American ideology." Cutting off and failure, let's keep these complementary themes in mind as Western man's admission of distress. America is just one case, a pretext, because in fact America's misunderstanding of its industrial and democratic paradise connects us, those of us from Western European culture, to the universal misunderstanding, established all over the planet.

I do not believe in the American anthropological singularity, in a humanity that would have swept away the age-old condition of the species by inventing an individual no longer separated from his life practices by the speech which institutes him. Ideology—at base, a neologism bequeathed to us by good old Destutt de Tracy in the eighteenth century!—ideology, I would say, is an ephemeral, functional belief, equivalent to a theology of consumption, a religion of a low period, which is to say, quickly worn out and today considered disposable, although capable of sustaining the illusion of several generations. These generations wait for other mirrorings, other discourses coming to renew the promise of man reconciled, no longer cut off or separated but living a life from which failure would be banished. I am of the opinion that Wiseman knows too much about the human condition to be surprised by it. I think his disillusioned remarks express his nostalgia, his melancholy as a subject faced with despair, with scenes of sorrow mixed with comical anecdotes, which he discovers with the innocence we share with him.

But deep down, in the depths of this big idea that highlights the absence of a way out, the institutional imperative that carries American society as well as the rest of humanity, what can such a cinema teach us? Wiseman's films are silent films. By that I mean—if I am to trust my impressions on initial viewings—that we enter these films with the sense of having pushed open the door of a monument, where the person walking through it hears the echo of his own footsteps. We enter a sort of echo chamber. The auteur says nothing. The viewer meets Totality, and sees it as his own world.

Glimpses of Totality? This familiar and terrible word evokes law, its application, its transgression, the indiscernible finality of everything, the enchainment of man to life, to pleasures as well as unspeakable miseries. We can see the institution and the innumerable masks of power to sort through, but they are always inseparable from the theater of the word. From the relentlessness of a production line in *Meat* (1976) to the efficient repetition of the buy/sell scenario in *The Store* (1983), from the strange routine of ski lovers in a winter resort in *Aspen* (1991) to the methodical lessons regarding the legal capacity to kill in *Missile* (1987), an enormous parade of discourses unfold, to exclaim, explain, notify, enjoy,

worry, convince, say . . . to say, indefinitely. But to what point? Is there a limit? Where is the wall of the word? It finally appears, patent, massive, and yet denied as a sign of humanity in this comedy of scientism that *Primate* (1974) allows us to glimpse, where a colony of scholars strive to conquer the frontier that separates us from the superior apes. We are there at the border, between science and a collection of outtakes, between the effort made again and again to broaden the space of the human prison and the fascination exerted by the pomposity of thought, the temptation of belief in a power no longer based in language but presented to man as being pure conditioning, for being brute essence.

An Iconic Cinema: On La Danse

I am reminded of Mallarmé's assessment of the dancer as "a poem set free of any scribe's apparatus."[4] I borrow this appraisal to express the *je ne sais quoi* that is resistant to commentary, an insurmountable disorder when it comes to translating into words the bodily "writing" of dance, this ceremonial form subjected to the order of the theater.

Carried by his poetic instinct, Frederick Wiseman takes this Mallarméan retreat, which has allowed an exceptional encounter, stunning in France, between an unembellished cinematic work and the savoir faire of

The Store. 1983

the administration of the Paris Opéras, facilitated by the mind of a filmmaker with knowledge of all things choreographic. "A gift to the public that they can *feel* without any explanation." This orchestral remark that Brigitte Lefèvre addresses to the dancers of the opera's ballet company speaks volumes on the spectacles of dance.

As an unconditional ally of the Mirror, the implacable guide to the dancers in rehearsal, Wiseman lets the images speak for themselves. But by virtue of editing, he transports them into this free zone of aesthetic commerce, where what is played out through the solicitation of an ephemeral spectacle is this lyrical component that reanimates in each of us the *passion of being another*—being this or that person, alone or in an embrace, being the couple in the scene. The rehearsals in the studio, privileged space and time where the camera tries to follow the lessons of the ballet masters, then cease to be the "behind the scenes" of the representations to come in the opera's grand theater, placing before our eyes the work of metamorphosing bodies into icons—body-images, themselves visual art, moving forms that hesitate and strive for perfection, to the point of eliciting in viewers this fervor that is part and parcel of the theater, which the ancient Latins called *pietàs*.

La Danse—Le Ballet de l'Opéra de Paris (2009) spotlights a peripheral question: how can theatrical dance exist? By that I mean: what are the strings holding up this marionette? As infatuated with objectivity as we are in the West, it escapes us that the organization, more precisely, the philosophy of the organization, could have a place in a film on dance, and not in the documentary mode but as the condition of the tableau. The ideologues who combat or look condescendingly upon classical theater assassinate thought, but the managers of Mass Entertainment have never managed to reduce the administration of a spectacle to financial investment, much less the manipulation, pure and simple, of a crowd prey to effusiveness. Wiseman's film reestablishes the primary truth of the human connection to the theatricalization of bodies, with, we might say, a Balzacian knack: by showing the administration as a function—a function of support (here the support of the aesthetic construction), which supports itself with the personality of its members and the context of an institutional history (in this case, of French manufacture, with its strength and its tics). Under the camera's gaze, the administrative sequences become a painting of characters.

A body of work crystallizes a way of thinking. What distinguishes Wiseman in the world of the documentary is that he has conquered a style, because his films have a direction; they think. And Wiseman writes his work in an ascetic mode, like someone who knows the price of saying things simply.

Wiseman invites us to reflect on the genre he has chosen: the documentary. I like the word, with its implicit *doceo*, which means in Latin, I teach, I instruct, I train by example. A documentary should retain the mark of a tight essay, should assimilate the stumbling and make a place for the preliminaries, for the study, as we say in painting. It is a cinema that offers itself to inventors of style. In an age of media encumbrances, heavy conformism, and facile rhetoric, Wiseman's lesson, laborious and never insistent, seems to me to be intensely topical. And, above all, I retain this from him: the whole art of the documentary is to leave the question open.

This text is an updated version of an essay published in the December 1996 issue of Les Cahiers du Cinéma. *Translated from French by Jeanine Herman*

1. Ernst Jünger, *Der Arbeiter*, 1932, in *Sämtliche Werke*, vol. 8, Essays II (Stuttgart: Klett-Cotta, 1981), p. 155.

2. In *Diderot's Early Philosophical Works*, trans. and ed. Margaret Jourdain (Chicago and London: The Open Court Publishing Company, 1916), p. 107.

3. T. S. Eliot, "The Metaphysical Poets," 1921, in *Selected Essays* (New York: Harcourt, Brace, and Co., 1932), p. 246.

4. Stéphane Mallarmé, "Ballets," 1886, in *Mallarmé in Prose*, ed. Mary Ann Caws, trans. Jill Anderson et al. (New York: New Directions Books, 2001), p. 109.

Juvenile Court. 1973

Boxing Gym. 2010

Racetrack. 1985

La Danse—Le Ballet de l'Opéra de Paris. 2009

Le Crazy Horse. 2011

Frederick Wiseman in Maine. 1997

Epilogue
Frederick Wiseman

Several years ago, when I was making a documentary film about dying patients in an intensive care unit at a Boston hospital, I wanted to shoot some sequences in the hospital morgue and was introduced to the man in charge of the morgue. He was responsible for the autopsy rooms and the refrigerators where bodies were kept prior to their retrieval by an undertaker. He was a pleasant, straightforward man who had been the administrator of the morgue for many years. I explained to him that I wanted to follow the procedure of the nurses who came to the dead patient's room, loaded the body on a gurney, and transported it to the morgue. I was particularly interested in how the corpse was concealed from visitors and patients on the trip. I needed his permission to shoot in the morgue and he quickly agreed. A few days later I happened to be in a patient's room when she died. After the nurses lifted the body onto the gurney and artfully concealed the corpse with sheets hanging over the side, I followed the three nurses from the eleventh-floor intensive care unit to the basement morgue, where they placed the cadaver in a refrigerator unit. I followed this procedure several times and was present on occasion when an undertaker came to claim a body.

One day I was invited to a "death conference." This was a regular meeting where the attending doctors would compare a diagnosis made when a patient was alive with the cause of death as determined by the autopsy. This conference was a regular part of the teaching program of the hospital. By the time I was invited to this conference my hypochondria was pretty much under control, since we had already been working at the hospital for several weeks. However, I was still slightly dismayed to see the liver, heart, kidneys, and pancreas on exhibit as I struggled to understand the technical scientific debate among the doctors as to the actual cause of death. I was also aware of the ease with which I accepted the routines surrounding death and how quickly I became accustomed to seeing dead people and their displayed body parts.

After six weeks at the hospital, the shooting of the film was over and I made the rounds to say goodbye to the staff physicians, nurses, administrators, and others who had assisted me and offered suggestions during the filming. I went down to the morgue to look for the man who had been so helpful and could not find him. I decided to write to him and went up to the hospital cafeteria for a farewell lunch with some members of the staff. Toward the end of the lunch I saw the man from the morgue at another table and walked over and thanked him for his help. He smiled, shook my hand and said, "See you soon."

This text originally appeared in the Winter 2004 issue of The Threepenny Review.

List of Works

Films

Titicut Follies. 1967
16mm, black-and-white, 84 minutes

High School. 1968
16mm, black-and-white, 75 minutes

Law and Order. 1969
16mm, black-and-white, 81 minutes

Hospital. 1969
16mm, black-and-white, 84 minutes

Basic Training. 1971
16mm, black-and-white, 89 minutes

Essene. 1972
16mm, black-and-white, 86 minutes

Juvenile Court. 1973
16mm, black-and-white, 144 minutes

Primate. 1974
16mm, black-and-white, 105 minutes

Welfare. 1975
16mm, black-and-white, 167 minutes

Meat. 1976
16mm, black-and-white, 113 minutes

Canal Zone. 1977
16mm, black-and-white, 174 minutes

Sinai Field Mission. 1978
16mm, black-and-white, 127 minutes

Manoeuvre. 1979
16mm, black-and-white, 115 minutes

Model. 1980
16mm, black-and-white, 129 minutes

Seraphita's Diary. 1982
16mm, color, 90 minutes

The Store. 1983
16mm, color, 118 minutes

Racetrack. 1985
16mm, black-and-white, 114 minutes

Blind. 1986
16mm, color, 132 minutes

Deaf. 1986
16mm, color, 164 minutes

Adjustment and Work. 1986
16mm, color, 120 minutes

Multi-handicapped. 1986
16mm, color, 126 minutes

Missile. 1987
16mm, color, 115 minutes

Near Death. 1989
16mm, black-and-white, 358 minutes

Central Park. 1989
16mm, color, 176 minutes

Aspen. 1991
16mm, color, 146 minutes

Zoo. 1993
16mm, color, 130 minutes

High School II. 1994
16mm, color, 220 minutes

Ballet. 1995
16mm, color, 170 minutes

La Comédie-Française ou l'amour joué. 1996
16mm, color, 223 minutes

Public Housing. 1997
16mm, color, 195 minutes

Belfast, Maine. 1999
16mm, color, 248 minutes

Domestic Violence. 2001
16mm, color, 196 minutes

Domestic Violence 2. 2002
16mm, color, 160 minutes

La Dernière Lettre (*The Last Letter*).
2002
35mm, black-and-white, 62 minutes

The Garden. 2004 [unreleased]
16mm, color, 196 minutes

State Legislature. 2006
16mm, color, 217 minutes

La Danse—Le Ballet de l'Opéra de Paris. 2009
35mm, color, 158 minutes

Boxing Gym. 2010
16mm, color, 91 minutes

Le Crazy Horse [working title]. 2011
HD video, color

Theater (selected)

Tonight We Improvise
by Luigi Pirandello
American Repertory Theater,
    Cambridge, MA
Director of Video Sequences and Actor,
    November 1986–February 1987

Welfare: The Opera
Story by Frederick Wiseman and David
    Slavitt, book by David Slavitt, music
    by Lenny Pickett
American Music Theater Festival,
Drake Theater, University of the Arts,
    Philadelphia. Director, June 1992
St. Ann's Center for Restoration and the
    Arts, New York. Director, May 1997

The Last Letter
An adaptation of the novel *Life and Fate*
    by Vasily Grossman
American Repertory Theater,
    Cambridge, MA. Director, May 1988
Theatre for a New Audience, New York
    Director, December 2003

La Dernière Lettre
Comédie-Française, Paris. Director,
    March–April 2000, September–
    November 2000
North American tour of the Comédie-
    Française production (Ottawa and
    Toronto; Cambridge and Springfield,
    MA; New York; Chicago). Director,
    May–June 2001

Oh les beaux jours (*Happy Days*)
by Samuel Beckett
Comédie-Française, Paris. Director,
    November 2005–January 2006.
    Director and Actor, October–
    November 2006
French tour of the Comédie-Française
    production (Cachan, Fécamp,
    Valenciennes, Villeurbanne, and
    Nevers). Director and Actor,
    January–February 2007

More information on Frederick Wiseman
and his work can be found on the
Zipporah Films website (www.zipporah.
com)

Biographies

Andrew Delbanco, Julian Clarence Levi Professor in the Humanities at Columbia University, writes widely about American literature and culture. His most recent book is *Melville: His World and Work* (2005).

David Denby has been a film critic at *The New Yorker* since 1998. Previously, he was the critic for *The Atlantic*, *The Boston Phoenix*, and *New York* magazine. He has written three books: *Great Books* (1996), *American Sucker* (2004), and *Snark* (2009).

Pierre Legendre is a historian of law, a psychoanalyst, and a proponent of "dogmatic anthropology." He is the author of many works.

Errol Morris is an Academy Award–winning documentary filmmaker. His films include *Gates of Heaven* (1978), *The Thin Blue Line* (1988), *The Fog of War* (2003), and, most recently, *Standard Operating Procedure* (2008). He lives in Cambridge, Massachusetts.

Marie-Christine de Navacelle is a film curator. She was director of the Cinéma du Réel festival at the Centre Pompidou from 1979 to 1989. She was subsequently in charge of audiovisual programs at the Ministry for Foreign Affairs in Paris. Since then, she has organized many cultural events in Japan, including retrospectives of Robert Bresson and Frederick Wiseman.

Jay Neugeboren is the author of seventeen books, including prizewinners in both fiction (*The Stolen Jew* [1981] and *Before My Life Began* [1985]) and non-fiction (*Imagining Robert* [1997] and *Transforming Madness* [1999]), along with three collections of award-winning stories. His most recent novel is *1940* (2008). He lives in New York City.

Geoffrey O'Brien's books include *The Phantom Empire* (1993), *Sonata for Jukebox* (2004), and *The Fall of the House of Walworth* (2010). His poetry has been collected most recently in *Early Autumn* (2010). He is editor-in-chief of The Library of America.

Christopher Ricks is William M. and Sara B. Warren Professor of the Humanities, and codirector of the Editorial Institute, at Boston University. He was Professor of Poetry at Oxford University from 2004 to 2009. His recent books include *Dylan's Visions of Sin* (2003) and *True Friendship: Geoffrey Hill, Anthony Hecht, and Robert Lowell under the Sign of Eliot and Pound* (2010).

Catherine Samie is an actress whose career was with the Comédie-Française, of which she was doyenne. She has interpreted the work of many classic authors, including Molière, Marivaux, Shakespeare, and Victor Hugo.

Joshua Siegel is an associate film curator at The Museum of Modern Art, New York, where he has organized more than ninety exhibitions, including *Frederick Wiseman* (2010); the gallery installation *Projects 84: Josiah McElheny* (2007); and *The Łódź Film School of Poland: 50 Years* (1999), for which the Polish government awarded him an Amicus Poloniae. With Kirk Varnedoe and Paola Antonelli, he oversaw a major reinstallation of the Museum in 2000 and coedited the accompanying catalogue, *Modern Contemporary: Art Since 1980 at MoMA* (2001).

William T. Vollmann is a novelist and a journalist. His latest book is *Kissing the Mask* (2010).

Acknowledgments

This book was made possible—and enriched—by the contributions of many friends and colleagues. We would like to offer our deepest gratitude to them.

At The Museum of Modern Art, we thank foremost Glenn Lowry, the Museum's Director, for his invaluable and generous support of this publication and the major retrospective of Frederick Wiseman's work that it accompanies, as well as the acquisition of thirty-seven new prints of Wiseman's films for the Museum's permanent collection. Rajendra Roy, the Celeste Bartos Chief Curator of Film, has championed this project as well, and we thank him for his wise counsel and enthusiasm. Our gratitude also goes to, in the Department of Film, Laurence Kardish, Senior Curator, Jytte Jensen, Curator, Charles Silver, Curator, Anne Morra, Associate Curator, Katie Trainor, Film Collections Manager, Peter Williamson, Film Conservator, and Sean Egan, Manager for their help on this project and for the warm collegiality and expertise they have offered over many years. Significant support has also been provided by Peter Reed, Senior Deputy Director for Curatorial Affairs; Michael Margitich, Senior Deputy Director for External Affairs; Nancy Adelson, Deputy General Counsel; Jennifer Russell, former Senior Deputy Director for Exhibitions; and, in the Department of Communications, Kim Mitchell, Chief Communications Officer, Margaret Doyle, Associate Director, and Meg Blackburn, Senior Publicist.

The Museum and Gallimard join us in thanking the authors for their insightful, erudite, and deeply personal contributions to this book: Andrew Delbanco, David Denby, Pierre Legendre, Errol Morris, Jay Neugeboren, Geoffrey O'Brien, Christopher Ricks, Catherine Samie, William T. Vollmann, and Frederick Wiseman. Gallimard, under the gifted leadership of Antoine Gallimard, Publisher, and MoMA's Department of Publications, under the gifted leadership of Christopher Hudson, Publisher, have been tireless, scrupulous, and expert in realizing this publication from inception to completion. We cannot do justice to the contributions of, at Gallimard, Colline Faure-Poirée, Editorial Director, and Hélène Quinquin, Associate Editorial Director; and, at MoMA, Kara Kirk, Associate Publisher; David Frankel, Editorial Director; Marc Sapir, Production Director; Hannah Kim, Marketing Coordinator; Amanda Washburn, Senior Book Designer; Robert Kastler and Rosa Smith in Imaging Services; and Rachel Spaulding, intern—but we thank them nonetheless. We are deeply indebted to Kyle Bentley and Octavie Dirheimer for their outstanding work in editing the essays, and to Victoria Mortimer, Jeanine Herman, Marie d'Origny, and Elise Nussbaum, for their elegant and spirited translations. And we are grateful to Stuart Klawans for his careful reading of the essays in manuscript and his astute responses to them.

At Zipporah Films, we thank Karen Konicek *tout simple*, for it is nearly impossible to know what to single out for special praise. We are grateful as well to Kasey Skeen for her invaluable assistance. At Idéale Audience, we acknowledge Pierre-Olivier Bardet and Nathalie Muller.

Joshua Siegel wishes to offer his personal thanks to Meredith Martin, Linda Burg Friedman, Marvin Siegel, and Mary Gordon for their kindness and encouragement in this as in all things. Better editors a writer could never have.

Finally, we thank Frederick Wiseman—for his brilliance, passion, tenacity, candor, and, it must be said, his killer eye and gallows humor. These are the hallmarks of his artistry, which he has also brought to bear on the creation of this book.

Joshua Siegel
Associate Curator, Department of Film
The Museum of Modern Art

Marie-Christine de Navacelle
Independent Film Curator